Bending Angels

Bending Angels

Living Messengers of God's Love

JACK H. EMMOTT

Carpenter's Son Publishing

Published by Carpenter's Son Publishing, Franklin, Tennessee

Published in association with Larry Carpenter of
Christian Book Services, LLC.
www.christianbookservices.com

Cover Design by Helen Mahnke

Interior Design by Suzanne Lawing

Printed in the United States of America

978-1-942587-75-0

To all of the Bending Angels in my life, especially my wife Dorothy and my grandson, Tristan, who at the age of three after evening prayers said, "God made Angels and Angels made Grandmas and PawPaws."

Acknowledgements

This book would not have been published without the angelic contributions of very special beautiful, gifted, well-developed and talented souls.

I give thanks to God for Dorothy, my wife and angel, for her typing, on evenings and weekends, the never-ending drafts of the pages of this book and for her honest, constructive criticism. She freely gave me the gift of quietness that an author needs to create a work.

My thanks to God for Sarah Cortez, my editor-poet, mentor and friend, whose art and discernment enhanced the strength and clarity of this work. To Ann Boland, my publicist, who is an encourager and insightful spreader of the good news. To Carol Wilhelm and Maureen Doherty, my intellectual property lawyers, who both gave me so much more than legal advice. To Gary Emmott, my brother-inventor-printer-entrepreneur, and Helen Mahnke, my graphic artist, who both insured that the cover of the book and the related Bending Angel Notecards echoed the beauty of the *Bending Angel* painting. To Justin Romack, my webmaster, who is totally blind yet sees more with his creative heart than a person with 20/20 vision. To my cousin, Allison Dawson, who has helped develop my digital life while my analogue existence remains challenging enough.

To Robin Schorre Glover and her husband, Hays, who generously gave of their time to encourage me to complete the book. To Robin for providing the iconic photograph of her father, Charles Schorre, in the book.

Thanks to three extraordinary, beautiful women who read the manuscript and offered their words of praise displayed on the back cover of the book: Lindsay Wagner, actress, author and the heroine known to many as the television's Bionic Woman; my cousin, Deanne Tilton Durfee, who has worked tirelessly around the globe to protect God's children from the devastation of mental and physical abuse; and, Debbie Adams, who has devoted her philanthropic talents, time, and leadership to care for thousands of children with cancer and their parents so that they may withstand the burdens placed on them by this horrible disease.

Last, my thanks to Stuart Bates, my minister, priest, and the Rector of St. Francis Houston, for his spiritual leadership, direction, and support

Thanks be to God, His angels, and these wondrous souls for giving life to this work and their love to me.

Amen.

Contents

Preface

There is an Angel who bends over every blade of grass, over everything and everyone who has ever lived. In my home on the wall above my bed, there is an Angel who bends over me. In my sleeping and in my waking, her presence is imprinted on my heart and in my soul. Over time, she has become an undeniable part of me. She gives me greater strength to become what God intended at my birth. She has given life and inspiration to every word in this book. Thus, you'll see her in her proper place on the book's cover.

Years ago in the mystery of time, my good friend and then Texas State Artist of the Year, Charles Schorre, painted her. With the creative gifts God bestowed upon Charles, he brushed her into existence with the mediums of water color and acrylic. To find her way into my bedroom, she made her own miraculous biblical journey through a flood in Charles' home. Then she was placed in a simple frame. Her image seems to leap off the paper into my daily life.

I have looked at her image in Charles' painting, entitled *Bending Angel,* so long and so often that I can see every pigment of her with my eyes closed. If Charles were alive now and I could ask his own thoughts about this work of art, he would say, "It doesn't matter what I think. What does she mean to *you?*"

So it is with this book, *Bending Angels,* and its stories of the Angels in my life who have bent over me in the swelling of my joyous heart with love and in unspeakable times of heartbroken pain. My Angels have uplifted me when

I could not find God or even myself in the midst of unexpected horror, tragedy, loss and separation from loved ones.

The painting's Bending Angel is as naked as we all are when we come into the world as God's creation from our mother's womb. She stands flat-footed, perched on a precipice with wings uplifted behind her shoulders. Her wings reflect God's promise to carry her safely as she prepares to fly down to earth to save another soul, to bestow another sacred message from God to one of us mortals who may be unaware of her presence. Or is she preparing to make her own leap of faith into God's loving arms?

The spiritual journey for us humans is, in a sense, a quest to find the sacred in the ordinary, to appreciate blessings as we move through our lives. It is also the opportunity to recognize God's Angels bending over us.

My hope is that this book, *Bending Angels*, will help you recognize those angels who have bent over you in the gift of days, months and years of the time on earth God has given you. May this book help you to see God's Angelic Spirits who come and go in your life, whether you appreciate their presence at the time, or whether many years must pass for those Bending Angels to be revealed to you as you study the layers of suffering and joy in your life.

After many years, I've come to believe that through the alchemy of sifting through the seemingly unimportant, transitory parts of a life, there may suddenly come the revelation of the glorious presence of Bending Angels and the realization that God has touched your heart and soul with His Eternal Love.

Many books have been written about Angels. The Bible is full of stories about Angels who came just as unexpectedly, mysteriously and suddenly as my Bending Angel to deliver powerful messages from God. Often times these direct messages were simple and acted upon with sincerity and passion by the person or persons who witnessed the Angel's presence. Through the ages of time, these stories of Angels have gained a powerful presence in our lives, even though they happened centuries ago.

Angels are not confined to the Biblical past. They are here and now because their work is not done. You see, God's love for us is not yet completed. We are not alone. God and His Angels have not abandoned us, although some are immediately recognizable and some are not.

So it is with my Bending Angels. Some announced their presence with the force of Gabriel's horn at the Lord's return to Earth signaling that Judgment Day is at hand. Thus, I recognized them immediately as the Hands of God or the Risen Christ touching mine. In certain other cases, more than forty years had to pass before I could come to appreciate what God did for me through Angels at times of great risk, hardship, and vulnerability.

The promise of life is also the certainty that death will follow. When we take our last breath and our hearts beat one last time, we all must make that one last leap of faith into the loving arms of God—just as my lovely painted Bending Angel is preparing to do.

When the promise of my birth has been fulfilled, I pray that I can do what Charles' Bending Angel does on the canvas. May I bend over in silence and prayerful submission on the last precipice of my life on earth and make that courageous leap of faith into eternity.

In reading this book, may you see Bending Angels in your own life. Perhaps you will see that you have been someone else's Bending Angel, joining others who have brought salvation, joy, comfort and peace to the human race as you seek to share God's everlasting love.

Charles Schorre, Texas artist

CHAPTER ONE

An Angel Leads Me
to the Dollhouse

In August 1954, instead of making my way to first grade, I made a different journey. My bicycle with its training wheels was left in my parents' garage. My Roy Rogers lunch kit and Dale Evans thermos gathered dust on my mother's kitchen table. The usual back-to-school purchases of a Big Chief writing tablet and number two pencils were now useless to me.

I was stricken with polio and paralyzed from the neck down at the age of six. My life from that moment became a quest for finding connections to myself, to those I loved, to my friends, and to my God. Connections to all those orphans of brokenness within me.

My journey was to Hedgecroft Hospital in Houston, Texas—a city struggling with a growing epidemic of *poliomyelitis*. There, in a makeshift classroom, I and the other children had daily lessons to try to keep our young minds alive and hopeful when our bodies were wastelands in the wake of paralysis and despair.

A dollhouse sat on top a cabinet in the rear of our classroom at Hedgecroft Hospital. Some of us in wheelchairs
and others on gurneys faced the teacher. All of us were paralyzed children of God, in ages ranging from six, like me, to
eighteen, like the girl across from my chair with pale skin,
an expressionless face, and useless limbs.

She looked at the blackboard with deep-set eyes. Her
blonde hair cut as short as her dreams of dates, dances, and
a senior prom. Her focus, like mine, was supposed to be on
the words spoken from the teacher's lips and on the lessons
and examples written in white chalk on a blackboard that
mimicked the darkness we were all facing.

This unnamed girl, who I never saw again after I left the
hospital, is still framed in my memory. We sat in class each
day in the same place over a period of eight months. Yes, we
held the superficial poses of interested pupils. But I knew
she and I were always somewhere else—a place where souls
dwell after being uprooted from the commonplace, the familiar, from our families by an unexpected catastrophe.

I must have spent half my days in class staring at her—not
that a boy my age found her attractive. Rather, I looked at
her hauntingly, wondering if she was who I might be when
I reached her age. Would I still be in a place like Hedgecroft
when I was in high school? Such morbid thoughts are not
ones that any child of six should have to dwell on. I tried
not to stare at her, not to envision the picture of my future
that kept popping up in my mind like air bubbles on the
surface of salty water from oysters in Tres Palacios Bay near
Matagorda. Like a good boy, I tried to look forward to the
front of the classroom, but all I could see was the life behind
me that would never be the same.

As the days, weeks, and months passed, my eyes kept
drifting from the high school girl to the teacher, then to

the blackboard, and then to the two-story dollhouse on the right on top of the cabinet in the back of the room. My eyes were drawn to it like iron shavings to a magnet. At the end of my class on most days, I asked the teacher or hospital orderly to roll my wheelchair to the back of the room so I could sit next to the dollhouse. It was holding something in me captive.

I remember feeling silly sitting there, for I was a boy and only girls played with dollhouses. I felt stupid and frustrated because I could not lift my hands to reach into the house to rearrange the furniture, the rugs, or the artwork which hung on the walls. But whatever quality or spirit the dollhouse possessed was strangely stronger than the negative thoughts I had of embarrassment, stupidity, or uselessness. You see, at the end of every class an Angel's voice beckoned me to sit with, study, and contemplate that house.

Gradually, I began to see and appreciate that dollhouse in ways I could never have imagined. The outside of the house was painted green and gold. The roof and sides sparkled with glitter glued on by the careful hands of an unseen artist. Little pieces of straw were also glued on its roof. Rhinestones were affixed to the outside of the house. I remember thinking that maybe those stones were hard and strong like diamonds. How I wished I was like that, instead of warm and fragile, too easily broken by the forces of nature beyond my control. I knew diamonds were formed and strengthened with heat, but the fever of polio separated me from those I loved and weakened my muscles.

After many weeks of viewing the dollhouse in passive silence, one day a realization struck me hard on the heels of hurt that this dollhouse was not just any house. As I gazed into its rooms, I saw my own home in Emmottville.

My body had been emptied of its strength, just as this

dollhouse had no people in it. I looked into its kitchen and smelled my mother's cakes and pies, the smell of bacon and eggs cooking on the stove. I could hear the sounds of knives scraping the sides of the metal bowl as Mommy cut the butter, sugar, salt, baking soda, and Crisco into the flour to make the crust for my favorite cherry pie.

I looked in the living room of that dollhouse and missed the laughter of my mom, my dad, my brother Charles, and my sister Carolyn Jean, as we watched the Milton Berle, Jackie Gleason, or Phil Silver shows. I missed my own bed, its mattress as comforting as my mother's caress, and even missed my father's scary stories read to me at bedtime. I remembered the chenille bedspread that had kept me warm in the cool of morning. I wanted my favorite chair—one with legs, not wheels. I looked in the dining room and longed to sit around the dinner table saying Grace with those I loved and who loved me.

The furniture in the dollhouse was beautifully crafted by the hands of a careful carpenter. His craftsmanship reminded me of the objects of pleasure and joy my dad had made for me and my siblings: the swing set, the see-saw, the slide, the hobby horses, and the stick ponies.

I wondered how different my childhood home was without me. Did the members of my family ache for me the same way I grieved their loss to me?

That school year at Hedgecroft Hospital in a makeshift classroom I was supposed to learn about reading, writing, and arithmetic. Instead, I learned much harder lessons.

Listening to an Angel's voice, I learned how to look into that dollhouse and see beyond the emptiness and loss, and to be thankful for the memories of love I received from God in the gift of grace—memories of my parents, my family, and my childhood home. I learned that what heals every wound and what makes every house a home is love.

Scripture says that the Lord's house has many rooms. Every child of God has a room in God's house; every soul has a place in God's Kingdom. Physical appearance, deformity, scars, and loss do not matter. Each child is special and has a place called home.

Beyond the beauty and poignancy of my childhood home in Emmottville, beyond the dollhouse at Hedgecroft and the unnamed high-school girl in my class, there—unseen by me—must have been the glory of God's grace calling me to enter the Lord's House, asking for me to become a part of the fullness of God's love, where emptiness and loss, joy and sadness, tears and laughter, darkness and light are all the same. There, we are all complete, beautiful, and beloved children of God who have an eternal heavenly home.

All I am, all I am not, and all I will ever be are God's. But it is also equally true in God's Kingdom that all you are, the promise of your precious birth, the hope you represent to the world, your love, life and the living of it, are God's also.

You may be in a chair with legs; I am in a chair with wheels. But to God we are the same. We are all going to the same place.

Who are we? Children of God. Where are we going? To the Kingdom of Heaven.

As you travel in the days and weeks and years ahead, remember that your greatest goal in living and loving to the fullest is to be on the lookout for the treasure which lies in the darkness, like the dollhouse was for me. To God and all of His Angels, a catastrophe, a death, a loss or a broken relationship is an invitation to step out of the darkness and into the light of God.

A home where the sweet sound of laughter is heard above the cries of human sorrow. A heavenly place where those we have loved and lost are waiting for us to embrace our grief, to dream our lost dreams, and to see our scarred and broken bodies as whole, as perfect, and as luminescent as the evening snow in the light of the moon.

In the classroom at Hedgecroft Hospital, an Angel said to me, "Jack, have faith. Step into the darkness. Open the door. Come inside. God will illumine your path. God will lead you home."

CHAPTER TWO

The Gift of Bread

As I lay for months in the bare hospital room at Hedgecroft Hospital, I ached for my family and my childhood home. I could only see my parents twice a day for twenty minutes. The undecorated hospital room offered little comfort and no entertainment. I lost all my expectations of ever playing with friends or going to a regular school. The silence was only broken by the screams of children I didn't know in a nearby examination room when a doctor inserted a long needle into their spines to tap fluid to test for polio.

I remember lying there looking through the window-panes of my tears and grieving for all the people I missed and all that I had already lost. *Why had God forgotten me?* After all, I was a good boy. *Where was God?*

Then, unexpectedly, God sent me an Angel. In the midst of my fears and unanswered questions, "Am I going die? Will I ever go home?" God sent me Great Aunt Mabel, my grandmother's dear sister. She came to visit me on her way to volunteer at St. Luke's Episcopal Hospital. Because of Hedgecroft's strictly enforced visitation periods, I had become despondent and bewildered as to why my own mom and dad were not continuously at my bedside. As a hospital volunteer, Auntie in her Blue Bird uniform, had special winged privileges to come at any time as often as God called her to be in my presence.

When she entered the room, I would be lying in a metal baby bed with tall side rails. I could not wiggle a toe or move a finger. There was a button to call a nurse, but I couldn't press the button. Ten other children were in the same room, but no one talked to each other. We were isolated from our families, from our previous lives, from every semblance of connection and hope.

Into this darkness, Auntie came with her radiant smile, carefully coiffed hair, beautiful gold jewelry, and perfectly applied make up and lipstick.

She brought such gifts of the spirit to me that she changed me forever. You see, into the darkness of crushing loneliness, doubt, and distance from all love, even God's, she brought a home-made, hot and fresh, little loaf of cinnamon raisin bread wrapped in aluminum foil. She even remembered to bring a small stick of butter. As she opened the foil, the steam and sweet aroma would fill my senses with all the remembrances of my lost home.

With one hand, Auntie would feed each morsel into my mouth while stroking my hair with her other hand. Her bread removed the taste of hospital food and the smells of the hospital's medicines, bedpans, and soiled sheets. Through her loving hands, I felt renewed; through the heavenly taste of her bread, I remembered all those who loved me and who I still loved.

Auntie's bread has long since been consumed. However, I can taste it even now. That bread from Auntie, like the life, death, and resurrection of Christ commemorated at Communion, fed me in the past and feeds me now in glorious memory. Just as the Body and Blood of the Risen Christ at the altar rail gives me a foretaste of God's Heavenly Kingdom, Auntie's bread gave me a foretaste of those rewards God had for me in this new life after the onset of my illness.

I imagine that there were countless other loaves of homemade cinnamon raisin bread that Auntie baked and gave to innumerable other small children of God at Hedgecroft and St. Luke's Hospitals. Those Godly gifts, administered with loving and sweet attention, made the world a greater reflection of the Body of Christ. Those who were sick like me, who prayed so hard to be cured, were not cured but rather healed, made whole from the inside out by a servant of God, by her smile, and by the yeast of her angelic love for life and for all of God's children.

Auntie lived 105 years. The bread of life, the Hope of Heaven, and her ministry were all baked in her kitchen. She taught me and many others four important angelic lessons:

1. Enjoy good food, and lots of it.
2. Always smile in the face of adversity.
3. Give hope to those in need of it.
4. Laugh. Laugh. Then, laugh some more.

When I remember Auntie, I often think that Jesus had a mother named Mary, who was a gift from God and who became Mother of all of us at Calvary. Auntie was a mother, not only to her sons, but to so many others. Lovingly spoken of as "Auntie," she was born and came to me in mystery and love from the Divine Womb of God when I needed her. She gave this love to many, many others. Because of her caring and nurturing stewardship in the name of Christ, that Angel to me at age six is surely a saint in Heaven now.

This Bending Angel's message was clear to me: "Let me show you the Love of God. Please taste the bread I bring to you. With these gifts from God, your spirits will be lifted. Your lungs will be filled with the Love and Light of Christ. Your aching heart will be healed with Heavenly hope."

CHAPTER THREE

If All Dogs Go To Heaven, Brownie Must Have Been an Angel

The spring of 1955 was full of hope and promise. I had returned home from Hedgecroft Hospital. On that first day back home, my father carried me in his arms upstairs to the bedroom I had shared with my brother Charles. As much as had changed within me, it was comforting beyond words to finally see the same wooden floor, to hear the familiar whirling sound of the Hunter ceiling fans above me, to rest my head on my favorite pillow, the same one Mom had placed under my head in the back seat of the car as I was taken to Hedgecroft Hospital the prior August. Charles' cork-based lamp with the revolving shade of cowboys, bucking horses, and circling wagons sat on the bedside table just as I had seen it last.

Once again I could take my turn "blowing out the lights" at bedtime as Mom flipped the light switch; I could kneel at bedtime beside my Mommy, Charles, and Carolyn Jean and say the Lord's Prayer. I did not mind that I could no longer climb the ladder to the upper mattress of the bunk bed where Charles and I slept. I was home.

On this particular day, I wore a pair of yellow shorts which exposed my legs including the braces I wore on my feet and legs. I focused on the sunlight which flickered through the leaves and limbs of the trees like the images of the home movies my father took. My father had carried me to a recently purchased redwood chaise lounge in the shade on the front concrete patio. I was six. My brother Charles was five.

Charles approached the chaise lounge. He leaned over and grabbed each of my feet with his hands. He had heard of my daily physical therapy in the hospital, I guess. Charles moved each foot and bent my knees towards my chin as if he was helping me learn to ride my bicycle again.

My grandfather PawPaw came over for a visit. He carried a bucket full of vegetables from his garden. But today, I was not interested in his vegetables, nor in the cigarette-burn holes in his clothes, nor in the false teeth he took from his mouth for me to hold, nor in his pants' cuffs full of cigarette ashes. Today, the thing of real interest was a small, brown, bobtailed six-week-old-puppy my PawPaw had brought with him.

Now, no one would ever mistake my PawPaw for a tender, loving man. His name would never be inscribed on the eternal wall of tolerance. Yet, he loved two things more than anything or anyone else in life: the game of baseball, and his dogs. And, here he was, giving me one of his dogs—a little, soft-brown puppy already snuggling into my lap.

I asked my mother and father if I could keep the puppy. Their answer was a prompt "yes." Without the results of modern scientific studies, my PawPaw and my parents knew the healing properties that a dog could provide to the ill, to the heartbroken, to the lonely, and to me.

PawPaw asked, "What name are you giving your puppy?"

"Brownie," I replied.

Thus, we began, this small, wiggling bundle of happiness and I. Brownie was a strange mixture of a dog. He had short brown fur with a white spot on his chest in the shape of an apple with a stem on it. He had deep, dark brown eyes that already looked at me as the hero of his universe. Looking into Brownie's eyes, I always saw this awe. Yet, there was much more. Brownie's eyes held a lot of mystery for me too. There was something about the depth and the beauty inside those eyes which I could never fully grasp. Just as there were things about my condition with polio I could not grasp or understand. I felt that Brownie and his eyes were telling me something that would make better sense of my paralysis, if I could just figure it out.

From the age of six until I was fourteen, Brownie was my constant companion. In days filled with joy and light, he was my shadow-partner, trotting at my side never leaving me alone. In days of darkness, he illuminated my path. Brownie never barked at me like my parents did when I deserved a scolding. He sat in total acceptance of who I was, what I was not, no matter how I behaved (or misbehaved).

Our one-hundred-acre wood along White Oak Bayou was full of tall trees and tangled brush. Seeing poisonous reptiles like coral snakes, copperheads and water moccasins was a common occurrence. Once I had regained my ability to walk, I took long walks alone with only the aid of a cane and Brownie to watch over me. I had no walkie-talkie, no cell phone and no portable house phone to use if something happened to me.

Once, I fell in the woods about a hundred yards away from the house. Brownie began barking and ran home. He got my mother's attention. She knew it was strange that Brownie was at our front door without me. Then, Brownie led her to me. My mother helped me stand up. She brushed me off. (My mother did that a lot.) "You alright?" she said. "Yep," I replied. "Then I'll go back to my chores while you and Brownie play outside."

On many occasions, Brownie circled the path in front of my steps like radar with four paws trying to find the snakes. Sometimes, he would spot a copperhead. These poisonous creatures with leafy skin were perfectly camouflaged to prevent detection by the human eye. In contrast, Brownie had no problem sniffing them out.

I would say, "Sic' em, Brownie."

He would grab the snake in his mouth and shake the life out of it. Often times Brownie suffered snake bites on the mouth, lips, and face. He endured those wounds to protect me from harm, just as the Warrior-Archangel Michael would have done.

I cared for Brownie when he was severely swollen with puss oozing from his painful wounds. I worried that those bites might kill him; they never did. When I was troubled or lonely, or suffering from a fall, or wondering how things would turn out in my life, Brownie would sit with me and my pain. He gave me his persistent love and unconditional acceptance. Brownie embodied the fact that sometimes words are much less important than quiet companionship.

Brownie would do anything for me. He even went along with my irresponsibility when he agreed to eat my third-grade math homework. Despite Brownie's cooperation, "the dog ate my homework" excuse never worked with my homebound teacher, Dorothy Carlton.

Brownie accompanied my brother Charles and me to the school bus in the morning and was waiting there in the afternoon when we came home from school.

If I was good or bad, happy or sad, awake or asleep, behaving badly or being a good, respectful son, I was always good enough for Brownie.

Brownie showed me the importance of rest, of keeping things simple, traveling light, and being loyal. He was my friend too. Like a good friend, he seemed to smile whenever and wherever he greeted me. He wagged himself from his head to the end of his stump of a tail. His greatest joy was hanging out with me—just like any other good friend.

In Rod Serling fashion, one of my greatest fears following polio was falling down and being unable to get up, with no one ever coming to help me. That phobia was magnified when I saw the *Twilight Zone* episode "Where's Everybody?" in October 1959 in which every person in the world disappeared except for the sole actor in the show. There were no other people for comfort, companionship, or community. No form of life left. No birds. No other animals. When I felt those fears, I only had to turn and look at Brownie to know where reality was and would remain.

In the eighth grade I had surgery to repair a broken rod in my back. When I returned home to recover, my bedroom was downstairs on a couch unfolded into a bed. Earlier, I had made enough money from selling cinnamon toothpicks on the school bus to buy an early Zenith transistor radio—one of those that weighed a ton.

What more could a fourteen-year old boy need than Brownie and a portable transistor radio? As I lay in bed one evening, I heard Brownie bark in the garage. Every time he barked, the Zenith radio had loud, hissing static. I thought that was just a coincidence, but then it happened over and over again. That gave me goose-flesh.

When my father got home from work, I yelled at him from my bed, "Dad, please come here now to listen to something strange on my radio!" When my father came to my side, I told him that each time Brownie barked in the garage there was a hissing noise on my radio.

Dad frowned. "Bubba, I do not believe you," he responded. I pleaded with him to sit with me and listen. Surely enough, a few moments later Brownie barked in the garage. My radio hissed again. My father was convinced. The only scientific explanation we could make was that there was a short in the washer or dryer in the garage. The vibration of Brownie's bark caused an electrical short which was picked up by my radio. At this time in my life when I was so focused on prayer, on the power of God and the belief in miracles, I wondered whether there was an invisible, sacred spirit—some mysterious link between Heaven and Earth, God and me—inside Brownie, my four-footed doggy-transmitter, a conduit of God's love.

I should tell you that Brownie's appearance was a little different than most dogs since his tail had been bobbed. My PawPaw was big on bobbing dogs' tails. When one of his female dogs had a litter, PawPaw cut the tails off of the dogs with his sharpened knife. As far as my grandfather was concerned, long dog tails were undeniable proof that even God can make mistakes. From his viewpoint, tails just got in the way. They didn't really accomplish anything. That's why Brownie was left with a little stub of a tail about an inch long. Whenever Brownie saw me, he wagged that stub of a tail with the speed of a humming bird's wings. At least PawPaw had left him a little dignity to wisp and wag in the air. Just as Brownie made the best of the tail that PawPaw had left him, with God's help and with Brownie I struggled to make the best use of what polio had left me.

Brownie was the first real family member from whom I learned about death. Dad brought me the news. I was lying in that bed downstairs still recovering from surgery when my dad walked into the room.

Dad served the news up cold. He said, "Brownie is dead. Sorry, Bubba. He must have had a heart attack when another dog bit him on the neck."

I took my dad's word. I had no words in reply. I did not need to hear the details. We buried Brownie in the back yard under a water oak without a marker on his grave. The cross of his life, love, and death was planted in the hole left in my heart for him.

Angels perform many functions for God's greater purposes. In Brownie's eyes, in his presence, love, devotion, he did for me what God's Angels do. He watched over me, protected me, accepted me, and shared my pain. In so many inexplicable ways, he warmed me when I was cold.

In those deep set, dark brown eyes I see now what I only got a flickering glimpse of then, through a four-footed, brown-furred, floppy-eared, bob-tailed dog—the loving eyes of God.

God created him. PawPaw gave him to me. My parents allowed me to keep him. I held him in my lap and in my life for a little while until he left on his winged flight to Heaven. I so wish I could hold Brownie again or hear my bob-tailed Angel bark just one more time.

I have to trust, as we all do, that all my Angels and I will be reunited one day in the eternal reward of God's heavenly kingdom. Surely, there, Brownie will be warm in my lap again beneath the tall pines in the flickering sunlight of God's Love for us.

CHAPTER FOUR

Dorothy Carlton

From 1955 to 1959 when I was not at Hedgecroft Hospital with pneumonia, severe colds, or respiratory fatigue, I went to physical therapy from nine o'clock in the morning until twelve o'clock noon, Monday through Friday. After physical therapy, I pigged out at Prince's Drive-in. Those good-looking gals on roller skates could serve up a swell burger on a poppy seed bun, French fries, and an extra-thick chocolate malt—the dessert of all gluttons in Cow Town Houston.

One day as I dozed off in post-lunch lethargy in the backseat of Mom's 1954 Oldsmobile Super 88, four-door, Holiday hardtop on the way home, Mom said that a homebound teacher was coming to our house to start teaching me. Mom said her name was Mrs. Carlton.

"Why 'homebound'?" I asked.

"She is a teacher who goes house to house all over the district to teach students like you that are unable to leave their homes and go to school," Mom answered.

That did not sound normal to me. I asked, "When can I go to school like the other kids?"

Mom said, "When you are ready."

"When will that be?" I asked Mom impatiently.

"When Mrs. Carlton says you are." Mom's reply let me know not to ask her any more questions and that I better do what Mrs. Carlton expected of me.

During the five years of physical recovery after my dollhouse days at Hedgecroft Hospital, my parents did not want my mind to atrophy like my muscles had. At Hedgecroft, a teacher from Spring Branch ISD had come to a classroom where we were taken to her. Now, my classroom was at home. My Big Chief notebook and my number two pencils were dusted off. My parents acquired a brown metal classroom chair. It was placed on the screened-in porch. Under the seat I could place my books. I could even lift the desk top and place my writing tablet, pencils, and erasers in the storage well under it.

Shortly after the metal desk arrived and my makeshift classroom had been readied, I heard a car door slam shut in front of our home. Mom exclaimed, "Bubba, Mrs. Carlton is here." Mother opened the front door for her to step inside.

Mrs. Carlton walked in with a stack of workbooks in hand. I examined her from head to toe. Her hair was brown and shaded with strands of gray. It was curly but not too tight. It rolled above the sides of her ears and the base of her neck. She wore thick, dark-rimmed, plastic glasses with bifocal lenses that looked like the bottom of two Coca-Cola bottles. In an outfit that I would come to know well—high-heeled shoes, tan hose, a dress, bulky earrings and a necklace, she sat next to me.

She smiled and said, "Jack, your mother told me you are working hard at therapy to make your body as strong as possible. It is just as important that your mind must be as strong as possible. It needs exercise every day just like your body at physical therapy. Here are your weekly assignments. I expect you to do them. I will check your work. I will help you get ready for full-time classes, so you will be prepared."

For those years of home-schooling, Mrs. Carlton was the entire school district to me. By car, Mrs. Carlton took her classroom to the homes of her special kids. There was no special education school facility, so her classroom went from Bingle Road to the east, south to Clay Road, north to FM 1960, past what is the Champions area now, and as far west as the Nine Bar Ranch, a classroom as big as one hundred and eighty-six square miles.

Occasionally, Mrs. Carlton took me on field trips in her car. She might say, "Jack, it is such a pretty day, would you like to go for a ride?" or "There are some really interesting places I want to show you." There were lessons to be learned both inside and outside the classroom. Learning could be fun and not all work. She drove me to the Nine Bar Ranch where cattle were raised and shipped to market for meat to eat. She showed me the Addicks Dam and Reservoir, a man-made barrier to prevent flooding of the houses in which families like mine lived. Rice farms and ricer driers which put food on our table. A salt mining operation in Hockley, Texas out Highway 290 that fascinated me as I saw how salt was mined and ended up in the salt shaker on our table.

Dorothy Carlton loved me. I loved her too, except when she doubted that my dog, Brownie, had really eaten my math homework. You see, Brownie had a ferocious appetite for those untouched pages out of my math workbook. He learned well what I wanted him to do when I placed those incomplete pages in his mouth prior to Mrs. Carlton's visits. I could show her Brownie's actual teeth marks and the paper still wet with warm dog slobber. What a great dog and good friend Brownie was. Loyal to me even to the end of every unfinished school math assignment. Despite Brownie's cooperation, the "dog ate my homework excuse" never worked with my homebound teacher, Dorothy Carlton.

From ages six through eleven, from first through fifth grade at Fairbanks Elementary School, my mom and dad also gave me a taste of normalcy about what it was like to be a real student. Although attending full-time classes was not possible for me, at least one afternoon a week Mom took me to school to have a cafeteria lunch and attend a class or two. In those visits, the teachers treated me as something "special," not different, challenged, or disabled. Like the American Express card, paralysis had its privileges, except the interest was paid to me by my home room teachers: sweet Lillie Holbrook in first grade, Madeline Horne in second grade, and Effie Dell Hancock in third grade. Although those beloved teachers treated me as "special," I still felt different and much less lovable than my peers. Yet, those home room teachers, through their positive actions, expressed the belief I so needed that when the time came I could handle full-time regular classes.

Although I enjoyed my weekly visits to Fairbanks Elementary, I had Mrs. Carlton, a teacher who gave me one-on-one attention and who was always prepared to teach. Her being prepared to teach made me feel that I must be prepared to learn. Both teaching and learning take dedication. Mrs. Carlton never missed a day at home with me.

When I did something well, Mrs. Carlton rewarded me with a gold star. When I did not act responsibly, there were certainly going to be consequences for me. Mrs. Carlton had no problem giving me that unforgettable look of disappointment or disapproval, followed by stern words or an extra assignment. She held me accountable for the consequences of my irresponsibility so that, as a consequence, I would become a responsible adult.

As our time together as teacher and student was ending, Mrs. Carlton and Mrs. Jones, the mother of a fellow student with polio, Linda Jones, prior to Memorial Day took us to the Battleship Texas and the San Jacinto Monument. Linda and I knew each other from having physical therapy together. She had a light-filled smile despite using crutches under her arms to swing her heavy metal-braced legs forward one arc at a time in order to walk.

On that hot May day under the shade of a live oak tree, I sat at a picnic table alongside and across from fellow homebound students I had never met. A boy who was a bleeder. A cute but very awkward girl with cerebral palsy. An attractive blind girl. A boy who had only hands instead of arms protruding from his shoulders. (He was missing limbs because his pregnant mother took Thalidomide to prevent morning sickness.) As I ate a hot dog and potato chips and drank fresh lemonade, I looked at them.

I asked myself silently, *what was it like to live in fear that the slightest cut could cause that boy to bleed to death? What must it be like to be such a pretty girl and know others see the ugliness of her arms and legs moving out of step with each other? How will that armless boy ever dress himself or brush his teeth or pee by himself? What must it be like for that girl to be in the dark all the time and not see the beauty of the earth and all living things?*

Later, my teacher, Dorothy Carlton, gave me a photograph of us around the picnic table. It is black and white in contrast to the diversity of the students she served and the conditions they bore. Life would be as hard on us, her students, hard as the Battleship Texas' bulkhead next to our table. We needed a teacher like her to be strong and fight for our worth. If she believed in us, then we must be able to believe in ourselves.

When I spoke at the Cypress-Fairbanks ISD's dedication of the Dorothy Carlton Education Center in 1983, I looked at Mrs. Carlton who sat in the front row. I told her how privileged I was to speak as her former student. I related that I had found my words for this occasion and for her, my extraordinary teacher, just as I had begun my journey with her at age seven. You see, a few days prior to the dedication I had purchased some number two soft-leaded pencils and another Big Chief Writing Tablet with its highly-textured impressionable pages. I had taken the pose of her seven-year-old student and put the lead to paper. I heard within me the voices of her many students. The words came as effortlessly as Mrs. Carlton had seemed to know how to teach her pupils. Pupils, who some lesser educators may have thought were unteachable or not worth teaching. What could "they" do or accomplish in life with an education anyway?

Looking into Mrs. Carlton's eyes, I said "The crowning achievement of every great educator is overcoming ignorance and indifference with education and knowledge. Mrs. Carlton, it is true that you helped us learn reading, writing and arithmetic. But what you taught us every day was that you loved us as much as you loved to teach. You loved the unlovable. The not-so-easy-to-love. And the unloved. Mrs. Carlton, in your calling you taught us many lessons. No matter what our condition, we each were inherently worth receiving an education. Even though some of us were not fleet of foot. Even though we had our limits due to polio, cerebral palsy, blindness or birth defects, you showed us that the human mind and spirit are unbounded. Our dreams were more important than the gravity of our misfortunes or our worst nightmares. Attitudes limit humankind, much more than physical infirmities. Because of you, we have this Center to honor you. Because you honored me as my teacher, I became an attorney. I earn a living and support my family. I am a responsible citizen and pay my taxes. Because of you, all of your students, like me, are living monuments to your blessed body of work."

Mrs. Carlton was truly a great teacher. Great teachers, as she, love to teach, so their students, like me, will love to learn. As my teacher, she made me stretch my mind so that I might learn. As one of God's Angels sent to me, for five difficult years, she stretched and spread her loving wings over me. She shared with me her wisdom and her heart, so that I might teach others that Angels bend over us every day and every night. That in darkness and in prayer, if we listen with our hearts, we can hear God's message from them: "Bless you. You are my child. Be still in the darkness for I have not forgotten you. I have sent you an Angel.

"Follow the beat of your Angel's wings. The breaths you take move in unison with the flutter of your Angel's wings. The rhythm of your heartbeats is in harmony with the hymns sung by my choir of Angels and Archangels. You will be led out of the darkness and into the Light of my Love for you. Although you may have lost your health or those you love, they and I, your Eternal Father, have never lost sight of you.

"Your life is a gift. It is still my gift, no matter your condition or infirmity. When the gift I have given to the world in you and in your birth is ready to be returned to Me, I will send an Angel to pin perfect wings on you, so that you may fly home to Heaven and be whole once again and be one with me and with my Love, Glory and Grace forever."

Amen.

CHAPTER FIVE

Do Some of God's Angels Have Hoofs?

Years before I was born, PawPaw acquired Old Donk from her prior owner who said she was too old to be any good to him. My PawPaw got the better end of the bargain as Old Donk gave birth to twin donkeys the following year. Long after her hair had turned to silvery gray and her youthful zest had left her, Old Donk was an important permanent resident of Emmottville.

To properly appreciate Old Donk's name, you need to understand that my grandfather, PawPaw, always sought to live simply. This was especially true when it came to naming his barnyard animals and pets. Little effort was given to naming such an animal as a donkey. Thus, Old Donk was her name, even though she was female. Smokey, Popeye, and O.D. (for Old Dog) were his dogs.

Old Donk was indeed a fixture in our family neighborhood, like a cross on a church, the weathervane in the shape of a rooster above PawPaw's garden gate, or the gable dormers on the white wood Cape Cod, two-story home he had built in 1937 for his wife Jennie.

Old Donk was dependable. She was as dependable as PawPaw's roosters crowing at dawn. She had her ways—her comings and goings, just as we mere humans who lived in Old Donk's neighborhood had. Her nature had to be understood, nurtured, and respected by all those who sought to enlist her service either in front of a plow in the garden or under the saddle occupied by young, unsuspecting grandchildren.

Like my PawPaw, Old Donk had deep seated notions and unchangeable habits. Her strongest and most respected need was to be in her home, PawPaw's barn. The wisdom to know the location of home involved Old Donk's simple knowledge of geometry—the shortest distance between two points was always a straight line between the place at which Old Donk was set free from her rider and the barn she called home.

All of us cousins, including Howie, Bobby, and I, learned this painful lesson early in life, when such lessons were learned by the infliction of pain, some bruising, and quite a few abrasions. At the age of five, Howie, Bobby, my younger brother Charles, and I often gathered in the yard in front of Aunt Mabel and Uncle Howard's small, white, A-frame, one-story house. On such occasions, we were struck with Western-itis. You would have thought Poncho and the Cisco Kid, Roy Rogers and Dale Evans accompanied us. Cowboy hats with hurricane straps. Cap pistols. Peppermint cigarettes. Boots and spurs. Bandanas around our dirt-ringed necks, often referred to in the South as "grandma-beads".

Playing Cowboys and Indians was not enough for us that day. Cousin Howie saw Old Donk walking by his house making her usual rounds on her way back to the barn. Howie grabbed a piece of white Rainbow bread to lure Old Donk his way. Old Donk's soft, wet, enormous, hairy lips wrapped around that slice of bread. At the same time, Howie slipped the noose of his rope around Old Donk's neck.

Howie cried out to Bobby, "Go get the saddle. Hurry! Don't forget the bridle too."

At this point, I started to get the feeling that we were all in trouble.

Reluctantly, Bobby asked Howie, "Why?"

Bobby knew he was not about to ride Old Donk unless a strong uncle was there to hold the reins. Bobby moaned and groaned but still got the saddle and the bridle. Howie and Bobby put the saddle and the bridle on Old Donk as if they had truly mastered the art. I should have known better.

Old Donk seemed to tolerate this ordeal pretty well. Instinctively, Old Donk knew how this story would end, unlike Howie, Bobby, Charles and me. Howie tied up Old Donk to the tree in front of the house. Now it was time for the big decision to be made. Who would have the courage (or the stupidity) to ride Old Donk first? Charlie stepped back under a tree. He wanted no part of this adventure.

I said, "Howie, you ride Old Donk first. You're bigger and stronger than we are. Anyway, you live closer to Old Donk and spend much more time with her than we do."

Howie responded, "No, this was my idea. I've taken the trouble to get Old Donk saddled up and ready to go. I'll go second. Bobby, you go first. You show us how big you are. Then we'll each have our turn."

The debate went on between us three cousins for what seemed an eternity. I realized that there would be no more fun that afternoon until this chapter had been completed.

Howie and Bobby said to me, "Bubba, you get on up there. We'll be right here beside you. We'll hold tightly on to Old Donk's reins."

I took leave of my senses and agreed to be the first rider. Later I found out why Bobby and Howie were so reluctant to ride Old Donk first. They had already learned their lesson but declined to share it with me, for reasons which soon became obvious.

As I mounted Old Donk, I noticed the strap underneath her stomach appeared to have a lot of slack. In fact, it looked as though one of my boots could fit easily between the strap and Old Donk's belly. I said to Howie and Bobby, "That strap looks too loose. Are you sure it's tight enough?"

Howie replied with the authority of a Texas Ranger, "Sure, we're sure. Don't be stupid. You get on up there. You'll be just fine."

I got up on top of Old Donk. That's when the trouble started. At first, Old Donk began walking slowly towards the barn. Then, she moved a little faster with each step. Bobby and Howie held on to Old Donk's reins. At this point, gravity took over. Gravity is an irreversible and indisputable law of the Old West. The saddle started to turn like the dial of a clock. First, I was at one o'clock, and then at three o'clock position. Then I started screaming. I found myself upside down in the six o'clock position with my head about three inches from the gravel road.

When I started screaming, Bobby and Howie let go of the reins to try to rescue me. Old Donk finally had us where she wanted us. That's when Old Donk decided to run that straight line I mentioned earlier. She sharply turned the corner toward the barn. I realized I had only two alternatives. I could ride Old Donk into the barn and get my head struck by a tree stump with a number of my appendages looking like broken branches, or I could surrender myself to the fate that gravity quickly takes all people in my condition—to the ground. The hands of an Angel must have been with me that day because when I let go of the saddle, both my boots came out of the stirrups. If they had not, this story might have had a tragic instead of a humorous ending.

With all the air knocked out of my lungs, I looked for my cousins through the dust of Old Donk's flight. I cried out to Bobby and Howie for help and sympathy. Instead, I saw my two cousins, who were to blame for this outcome, rolling on the ground and laughing uncontrollably at my plight. Charles was still standing under the same tree not knowing whether to laugh or cry at the events he just witnessed.

* * *

In our relationships with those we love, we often take things for granted. In fact, it is all too easy to do so. Yet, everyone has basic needs and routines that need to be respected and appreciated. On too many occasions, we try to change those we love, we try to change their rituals, routines, and even their basic natures.

PawPaw's Old Donk had her needs and routines that etched my heart in ways that are difficult to express, but let me try. For instance, one of Old Donk's most endearing daily rituals was her quest for daily bread. Her search for daily bread seemed to me as sacred as receiving the sacraments at St. Francis Episcopal Church, except Old Donk received her bread on four hoofs. I received mine on my knees. I never ran up to the altar rail to receive the Holy Host, the Bread of Life. Likewise, Old Donk was not about to rush around our neighborhood to receive such nourishment for her body or her soul. Instead, she walked out of the barn early in the morning past the row of live oak trees and up the circle gravel driveway to the backdoor of PawPaw's porch. As PawPaw stepped out the backdoor and put out his Camel cigarette, Old Donk would be there with her hunger. PawPaw would chuckle and place a piece of toast in Old Donk's mouth. She chewed that toast like PawPaw's cows chewed their cuds.

Then the ritual continued. She made her way through the woods to our house and stood by our backdoor near the kitchen until someone noticed it was time for bread. After she received the bread from Mother's warm kitchen, she moved on to Aunt Betty's and Uncle Hewett's house, then to Aunt Virginia's and Uncle Robert's house, then to Aunt Mabel's and Uncle Howard's house, then to Aunt Julie's and Uncle Tom's house, and then to Uncle Donald's and Aunt Marie's house, until the daily ritual had been completed. After this ritual necessary to her existence in Emmottville had been satisfied, Old Donk leisurely made her way back to her home in PawPaw's barn.

It seemed as though receiving her daily bread in this manner was a sacred way for her to earn her right to go back home. The aroma of bread was her compass. The taste of bread was her life.

One day in the mid-1960s, Old Donk did not show up at our back door. I knew something was terribly wrong. Old Donk's daily visits had been comforting, predictable and unchanging for me in sharp contrast to my health with polio. Old Donk died that day, but certainly not the memories nor the invaluable lessons I learned from her. Lessons I needed as I maneuvered through a life irrevocably changed by an illness so few understood, including me.

Dusting off the memories of her now, I can think of a few more lessons. Routines and rituals are important amidst the changes, the ebbs and flows, and partings in our lives. No matter if it was windy, rainy, icy, cold, or blazing under a hot summer sun, Old Donk was committed to her ways and her comings and goings. As God's four-legged Angel, in her own way, she was telling me and all those in her neighborhood that the ordinary, daily experiences and routines that are observed are as sacred and important as anything else. We should respect that and give thanks to God for that in the lives of those we love and in ourselves as well. When we are empty, broken, or seem to be wandering aimlessly in life, waiting to catch our next breath or see a glimpse of Heaven, maybe it would bode well for us to bend our knees and find the Bread of Eternal Life, the taste of Heaven.

The day Old Donk died, PawPaw pulled her body out of the barn with his Pony tractor. In his two-toned, white and orange, two-door Chevrolet with three dogs in the back seat, PawPaw picked up Howie, Bobby, and Charlie. I could not go with them as I was confined to bed recovering from surgery. PawPaw drove them to where Old Donk was to be put to rest in the ground. A rectangular shallow grave was not good enough for our beloved Old Donk. No, she deserved something much better. So Howie, Bobby, and Charlie took their shovels and outlined Old Donk's body on the surface of the ground–to dig a grave that respectfully and perfectly fit her body. After Old Donk's body was placed in the donkey-shaped grave, Charlie noticed something was very wrong. My sweet brother Charlie said, "Everyone stop the burial. There's no place for Old Donk's ears!" Charlie held up her burial to dig out a place in the ground to put Old Donk's long floppy ears. These were the ones she had used to listen for PawPaw's backdoor to open and close in the mornings to signal the bread she loved so much had arrived. The burial was made to wait until all of Old Donk could be honored, embraced, and respected—from the tip of her tail to the end of her long, tender, floppy ears.

As Howie, Bobby, Charlie, and PawPaw lowered Old

Donk and her ears into the grave about forty feet north of the cottonwood tree by the old cedar barn, I wonder if they then, like me now, thought that one day we will all be like Old Donk. Those who loved us will one day bury us too and let us go back home to God.

Meanwhile, like Old Donk, we should keep on nurturing our nature and keep searching for the Bread of Life. Then, one great day we will taste the joy of Heaven as sweet as the memories Old Donk made for us.

Old Donk, God's Angel with hoofs, and all us children of God need that daily bread and the knowledge to find our way back home. A Bending Angel, like Old Donk, was surely sent to us by God. She said, "Follow my path and God will lead you to His home, a home you will have a foretaste of, with the taking of your daily bread."

Lessons Learned and Messages Heard From Old Donk

1. We each have our own nature that needs to be appreciated and respected.

2. Each living thing, animal or person, is sacred–a gift to us from God. Gifts and people should never be rejected. They should be cherished and shared. We could never make Old Donk into a Palomino pony. Why should we try to change those we love, their rituals, routines, and basic natures? Nurture nature. Conserve nature. Don't declare war on nature.

3. If we truly love them, we need to help others stay at home in the places they are most comfortable. We could never keep Old Donk locked out of the barn. Why should we keep our spouses, children, and kids from being in their sacred and most comfortable places and spaces?

4. Old Donk's greatness is not measured by a magnificent

stable, gold horseshoes, or a diamond-studded silver saddle. Her life and how she lived it with us were the treasures, her true worth. Likewise your home address, the car you drive, and the country club you belong to are not important. How your life reflects God's Love is.

5. Endless time is not measured by a clock. It is measured and observed in the simple, ordinary, daily routines of those who move in and around us each day–at home, at the office, or at the farm like Old Donk. It is in those timeless movements, as in daily prayer, that we remain stable and centered despite changes, separations from those we love, or being broken by disease or paralysis.

6. Take time to slow down each day and night to seek out, find, and savor your daily bread. Like Old Donk, open your eyes and listen with the ear of your heart to the Angels in your midst. Taste something sweet. Hug a friend. Hold hands. Dry a tear. Offer words of encouragement. Let the words of a prayer be heard falling softly on open wounds in need of healing. Say to someone you love him or her—all of him or her—the whole, the broken, the incomplete, the lovable, the unlovable, and the unloved.

7. Do those things which warm and comfort your soul–a cup of tea, a bowl of chicken soup, holding an innocent child in your arms. You will experience the sacred and the eternal. The spirit which God set in motion with your first heartbeat will fill the emptiness in other children of God. Nature abhors a vacuum. What do you fill your emptiness with? Alcohol? Work? Anger? Spending too much money? The Love of God?

8. Give someone else their daily bread, as my PawPaw gave

Old Donk a piece of leftover toast each morning on his back porch. You need not be a rabbi, minister, pastor or priest to do holy acts. Every word spoken deeply and honestly in love never dies, but remains sacred and eternal.

9. Live, love, and die in community. Find those who comprise a community of care. Hold hands and stay close to them—just as Old Donk knew how to be near her barn, the place she felt at home.

10. Just like my brother Charles dug a place for Old Donk's floppy ears as she was buried, we must make room for those we love on Earth as God does in Heaven. We and they deserve that respect.

Also, learning how to say goodbye to those we love is one of life's most important lessons. Old Donk showed me, my forty-five first cousins, eighteen aunts and uncles, my grandparents, and visitors that lesson. At my age, whenever I roll my wheelchair and sit quietly by the cottonwood tree where Old Donk was laid to rest, I sometimes think I hear the dusty shuffle of Old Donk's angelic hoofs passing by, etching deeper lessons in the pathways of my heart. Yes, God's Angelic messengers can have four hoofs.

CHAPTER SIX

An Angel for Wonder Boy Emmott

It was soon to be the summer of 1960. I was eleven and approaching the sixth anniversary of my initial fight with polio. For six long hard years I had been consumed with the desire to become the champion of health I had been when I celebrated a joint birthday with my brother Charles on August 12, 1954, two weeks before succumbing to the polio virus born from the murky flood waters of White Oak Bayou behind my childhood home.

Charles, age five, and I, age six, had blown out birthday candles on Mother's homemade chocolate cake that melted in our mouths like our hearts were melted by her lullabies at bedtime. Mother always carefully put a shiny dime in the cake wrapped in aluminum foil. This time, Mom cut a piece of cake for Charlie and for me. Each of us were rewarded with a dime, a shining silver coin denoting the bigger, deeper treasures Mother left for us in the memories of such loving moments.

Chocolate cake. Hand-cranked vanilla ice cream which

could put Baskin-Robbins out of business. Matching black cowboy hats with hurricane straps, fringed shirts, belts, boots, holsters, cap pistols, and peppermint Marlborough cigarettes. Such moments are recorded as vividly in my memory as the images in our old 8MM home movies.

This late spring of 1960 was different than any other, however. There was a distant calling of legendary spirits in the woods of Emmottville. Moss hung from the live oaks like fans in the outfields of baseball stadiums all over America, waiting to witness their heroes, past and present. There was an excitement in the country air. I could almost feel the presence of famous kindred spirits, like Warren Spahn, Nellie Fox, Babe Ruth, Shoeless Joe Jackson, and Ty Cobb, walking in our woods. Amidst the smell of honeysuckle vine and PawPaw's burning leaf piles, the aroma of ballpark popcorn and peanuts teased my nostrils as I watched my brother Charles, my sister Carolyn Jean, and my cousins Bobby, Howie, and Freddie fashion a makeshift baseball diamond in the front of my parents' yard. Boat seat cushions for the bases. Creosote posts and chicken wire for the backstop. The shade of elegant oaks and pine trees for a dugout.

From my earliest days, before and after polio, I believed I would one day fill the shoes of a great baseball pitcher who had once knocked off the cover of a baseball with a wooden bat. I was certain then that this gift, this calling, was imprinted on my soul and genetic material. You see, my grandfather, PawPaw, was not only named "Jack Emmott" like me. He was also the once acclaimed "Wonder Boy Emmott," who played in Houston for the Brunner Nine, and later for a company team of Cargill & Company, between 1915 and 1926.

I had grown up breathing this history. I knew that in

1917, Wonder Boy Emmott's pitching had enabled his team to win the Houston City Championship. Wonder Boy threw a knuckleball and a fastball that even attracted the attention of the St. Louis Cardinals. St. Louis offered him a job on their pitching staff in 1914, just prior to World War I. PawPaw asked his father for permission to leave home and join the team. His father ended that dream by simply but firmly saying, "No. There is no future or money in baseball. No family with constant travel from town to town, city to city." Even so, PawPaw had played a great part in Houston's early baseball history.

That summer PawPaw showed me his large callused hands and fingers and revealed to me the pitching secrets that the then sixty-nine year-old Wonder Boy Emmott never had forgotten. Polio was not about to be the death of *my* dream. I believed that miracles and inherent greatness are in each one of us through faith, prayer, hard work, and determination.

I had a glimpse of such an affirmation one afternoon on his porch as PawPaw showed the ragged-edged, water-stained newspaper clipping from the *Houston Press* of October 1916. The article reported a game that PawPaw must have reenacted in his mind countless times under lazy oaks as he planted fruits and vegetables in his white picket-fenced garden.

Only four players on the Brunner Nine showed up that momentous day while the Houston Oil Company team fielded a full roster of nine players. There was uproarious laughter at the sight of the mismatch. (The thought of me or my goal to play ball being a mismatch for polio never came to my mind that spring. That would come later.) On that day in October of 1916, PawPaw answered the laughter from the Houston Oil Company teammates with the kind of pitching and hitting that earned him that "Wonder Boy" title. The ninth inning ended with PawPaw's team winning the game three-to-one. The Brunner Nine beat all the odds, doing the impossible.

In April, May, and early June of 1960, I was not concerned about "the odds." I was consumed in a quest for the cure that I had prayed for, attended St. Francis Episcopal Church worship services for, made joyful noise to God in the Cherub choir for, attended physical therapy for five years for, had my body re-sculpted by a great orthopedic surgeon for, had steel rods placed in my back for, had thumb transplants to better grasp the bat for, crafted my own smooth oak bat on my PawPaw's lathe for, had my ankles broken and fused to wear those low-topped baseball shoes at the little league baseball field for.

By early June, I was openly bragging to anyone who listened that I was going to earn a place on the Little League team, just as my PawPaw had etched a place in Houston baseball history as Wonder Boy Emmott on the Brunner Nine. Only three short weeks were left before Coach Oscar Ochoa was to hold tryouts, and anyone who could play would suit out for the team.

After school and on weekends, rain or shine, hot or cold, I went out with my siblings, cousins, and friends, to practice, practice, and practice. No sacrifice was too great. I knew God would not let me down if I gave God my best. I knew every weakness in my body would be replaced with Godly strength. I had already experienced what hell was. It was not losing a baseball game. It was the nightmare of dreams that never came true. It was insensitive physical therapists who sought to kill my spirit of a cure or recovery by reminding me all that my paralysis stood for or against. I already knew heaven was not just having your wishes come true. It was experiencing unconditional love by those called family and friends.

Yes, my nickname was destined to become Wonder Boy Emmott, too. Foolish, wishful Bubba. Everyone knew the ending of this story as I was writing it with my daily rituals. I stood at home plate with my bat in hand. My cousin, Bobby, must have wanted to spare me disappointment at his hands. He threw pitches with a nice slow arc. I made contact with the bat. But by the week of tryouts, the ball I hit with all my strength only traveled twenty or thirty feet. I tried to run to first base, but my legs had the speed of a snail. The intentional fumbling of the ball by an infielder could not conceal that I would never have the speed of foot to beat an infielder's throw to first base. So, after a while with balls escaping my outfielder's glove, with my pitches falling short of the plate, much less the strike zone, I graciously accepted my sister Carolyn Jean's offer to bat for me, my cousins' offers to catch for me, and my brother Charlie's, offer to run the bases for me. After all, I just knew their help was only temporary. Everyone knew a kind of death march was on for my dream, except me.

At the end of our last neighborhood baseball practice, I left the field more alone than ever. Fear was as close to me as the baseball cap I wore on my head. In desperation, I muttered to Charlie that I was going to get a good night's sleep so I would be at my best the next morning when we walked together to the Little League field and claim our rightful places on the team. Charlie did not respond.

I knelt at bedtime and said my prayer of prayers. No matter what I had said to others, I knew that unless a miracle happened, the dream of Wonder Boy Emmott for a place on the team roster the next day was over. My dream would die. Those olden baseball spirits walking in the woods of our family compound would never hold the hands of a boy like me, who so much wanted to experience the greatness or even the acceptance he had lost by contracting polio less than a year before the 1955 Salk vaccine.

"Dear God, when I wake up tomorrow, please give me your miraculous cure. If Your Love and Spirit fed 5,000, raised the dead, made a blind man see, and healed a leper, surely You will answer my prayer. Please do not let me down. If Your Love heals all, then please heal me."

I asked my mother, "Do you think God hears me? Will I be cured when I wake up? Will I make the team?"

Mom looked at me and all my suffering. Mary, the mother of Jesus, must have looked at her Son 2,000 years ago as He walked His way to Calvary in much the same way.

She said, "Whatever God's reply, I know this, Bubba. God loves you and so do I."

I tried not to notice the tears in the corners of my Mommy's eyes. Tears that only a miracle could dry. Some men make their own crucifixions. Other times, disease does the evil. Our bodies get strung up. Our good health and hope get nailed to a cross.

The dew of the dawn of a new day came. I pulled off my covers and sat up. I saw the same old weakened arms and legs I had the day before. I got dressed and walked to the kitchen. I sat down on a bar stool at the breakfast bar. My mother stood on the other side of the bar at the kitchen sink. She could not make eye contact with me. Her back was all I saw as she faced the kitchen window washing the dishes. As if this was just another ordinary day, with her back to me, she asked, "What would you like for breakfast, Bubba?"

I did not answer. Food was not what I longed for. I asked her where my brother Charlie was. She did not reply. Her silence let me know that my brother had left for the ball-park without me—without saying goodbye, without saying that he was sorry God had not answered my prayer. The two turned backs of those who loved me, who could not face the pain, the death of my Wonder Boy dream. My eyes filled with tears.

I stood up. Without saying a word, I walked out the backdoor into the yard behind my house. The screen door swung shut. Part of me was left inside my childhood home. The hope fueled by love was no more. Grief overhung my head as if the pall was the canopy of the white and black oaks between the earth and sky.

For the first time in my life of recovery after polio, my grief was so dark, my loss so great, I did not care whether I lived or died. I collapsed and fell against the back of the house's reddish-brown, cedar-shingled wall and sat in a puddle of my tears. Sitting and leaning back against the wall, I did not care if I could not get myself up off the ground. I would stay there alone, undiscovered and help-less. Abandoned by God, if there really was a God.

A part of me died that day at that moment of dark rec-ognition. Yet that death was penetrated by the sound of the backdoor opening and closing. My mother walked toward me. She did not say a word. Her love for me left her speech-less. On my left, she sat down next to me. I looked at mom. Her face and mine were wet with tears. Our broken hearts shared in silence what words are wholly inadequate to pro-vide at times like these. It wasn't just not making the team, but being forgotten by God. My would-be teammates leav-ing in silence, the way the silent, invisible thief of the polio virus had stolen my health on the hot, humid, heartsick day on August 25, 1954.

I asked Mom, "How could God do this to me?"

She had no reply.

Mom and I sat there for the longest time crying tears with our arms around the grief we shared—the kind of moments that parents fear the most when they come to know that their child is not theirs at all, but God's. For, indeed, the mystery that fills the human vessel called body is the Holy Spirit that dwells within.

The wet mascara ran down my mother's cheeks. Only silence witnessed the mother and child clinging to each other and their commonality of suffering, each one's heart wounded in compassion for the other.

Then in silence, God's answer finally came. An Angel appeared. A holy message was delivered. To my right, a man stood looking down at me, appearing as unexpectedly as Jacob's Angel. It was Oscar Ochoa, the baseball coach. I looked at him with eyes asking, "What are you of all people doing here?"

He knelt beside me. He put his hand on my right shoulder. He handed me an unwrapped cardboard box. He said, "Bubba, all of us on the team wanted you to have this. God knows you've earned what's in this box."

I wiped away my tears and opened the plain cardboard box carefully to see what I expected least. A gift from God from an Angel of God. It was a brand-new, carefully folded team uniform. It said I was part of the team in spirit. At that moment, all I was, all I was not, and all I would never be, was really part of something after all.

My tears drowned out any words of thanks. I did not speak. Coach Ochoa left. Mom and I remained seated on the grass behind the house for the longest time. Later Mom helped me up on my legs. Silently and alone, I walked with the box into my bedroom and placed the uniform in the top drawer of my dresser.

In the days of adolescence which lay ahead, when I felt incomplete or not accepted because of polio, I went into my bedroom, opened that drawer, and looked and touched that uniform which came to clothe the loss I had felt that summer day. Was it the way Mary must have looked at the cross her Son was crucified on at Calvary after His body was taken down? Was it the way she must have held, caressed, and embraced the robe He wore before He was stripped of that cloth to die alone?

I never had the courage to put on that uniform or to look into the mirror and see the Wonder Boy Emmott that couldn't be. The pain of it was just too much. Yet that plain box was really wrapped with the kind of love that soon became a part of my healing. The gift of this Bending Angel said that I would be healed, not cured, by God's Love.

Through the Grace of God that spring and early summer, I found my limits without a single person telling me the foolishness or hopelessness of my dreams. If that is not God's Love, I do not know what it is. That same love brought the coach to my backyard to deliver a message to save me and my faith that day. It caused my brother and sister to fill the emptiness with the strengths they possessed and that polio had taken from me. That love caused Charlie to start first grade at Ridgecrest Elementary a year ahead of his time so that he could be in my public school classes and attend to my needs by running the bases of life which I couldn't feel beneath my feet.

I wish I could find that uniform. I would like to put it in a shadow box on a wall in my house. Yet, I would bet the uniform has long since turned into rags. The mother who grieved for me has died. I have lost my Warren Spahn, Willie Mays, and Roger Maris baseball cards. My bat and glove are gone.

Yet in its holiness, the uniform's presence today is just as real and eternal as the pain, poignancy, loss, and love that took place that summer long ago. Health could never be regained. A cure could never be found. But because of Angel Coach Ochoa the broken pieces of the life and the dreams of an eleven-year old boy with polio were made to fit and helped to heal by a simple offering in a plain cardboard box. No one could ever take that from me.

At the first, and most important, brokenhearted moment in the life of an eleven-year old boy, I received the kind of angelic love I needed most. Another of God's Bending Angels let me know I was not only a part of the team. I was surely a child of God also.

CHAPTER SEVEN

When You Need One the Most, God Always Sends You an Angel

It was the first Tuesday after Labor Day, 1960. I was a boy of twelve. My first fearful day of sixth grade had arrived.

This first school day had started at seven o'clock in the morning in my childhood home in Emmottville. The whole house smelled of my mother's breakfast cooking–eggs sunny-side up, honey-cured fried bacon, buttered toast–which my brother Charlie and I rapidly ate.

Charles and I quickly walked out the front door to Emmott Road. I had no time to waste—my short, struggling gait from polio took extra time and effort as we went down the oil-soaked shell road to the bus stop. I had to hurry to catch the yellow bus driven by Mr. Bubba Willbern.

To anyone on the outside of my life and struggles with polio, the destination of my daily school bus ride would be Post Elementary School. But as I learned that year, my daily bus ride was always and forever to be inexplicably headed somewhere else deeper in my heart and soul.

As Charles and I walked across the cattle guard, I saw the bus coming to a stop at the end of our road. I made it just in time. The bus door opened. I lifted my left leg up to the lower step of the bus. I stiffened my left leg and body so Charlie could push me up into the air to the left until my weakened right leg could swing under me by gravity alone. A pendulum amidst paralysis. An embarrassment of awkwardness viewed by a long line of onlookers at the windows on the bus. I felt like an ugly fish in a fish bowl. Then the leg-lifting process repeated itself up to the second and third steps until my two feet found the floor of the bus next to Mr. Willbern. There I stood, tired and very embarrassed. I felt unlike any other student on the bus. I was certain everyone on the bus saw that my left shoe was built up two inches higher than my right shoe. My legs were of different lengths. A bulky Milwaukee brace made of steel and leather was around my torso. The brace held me straight as my spine continued to curve with scoliosis. A white football helmet was worn on my head to protect the brain God had given me in the event my knees collapsed and my head crashed to the floor.

As I looked down the center aisle for an open seat, all the seats on the left were taken. Where would I sit? Fearing rejection and indifference, I asked myself, "Who would want to sit next to me, a crippled boy?" I looked with anguish to the other side of the bus for a place to sit.

Then, something unexpected occurred. On the right on the sixth row of seats, I saw a sweet little girl smiling at me. She did not look away from me like the others did. She moved closer to the window. With her right hand she patted the seat next to her inviting me to sit beside her. She looked about seven years old with wavy brown shoulder-length hair illumined with highlights from the summer sun. Her skin was tanned from playing outdoors; her eyes were as blue as the waters of the Cayman Islands. Her spirit was as peaceful, poised, gentle and cooling as a soft summer breeze on a warm afternoon. She wore a brown skirt with a plaid cotton short-sleeve blouse with a Peter Pan collar, brown leather shoes, and white cotton socks.

I sat right next to her.

"Hi. I'm Cheryl."

"I'm Jack," I replied.

"I know you. You are the boy who has polio like my Aunt Margaret did," she said.

I looked into Cheryl's face again. I saw much more than a pretty, younger girl on her way to class. I unexpectedly felt whole again, like before I had polio. I somehow knew she saw me as a whole person, a child of God, and not as a crippled boy. That is the way I believed that God saw all children. *"Jesus loves me. This I know, for the Bible tells me so."* Cheryl seemed to have that way of seeing me just as I saw her.

Now that I am much older, I often wonder if children as young as Cheryl are nearer to God's heart. As we grow older do we forget that gift? Do we start paying attention to the meaningless and superficial differences between people?

That school year, every time I got on the bus and saw her face, there was no one else on that bus except Cheryl and me. Those precious minutes together each day held more power over me than the risk of rejection by my peers or the fear I had of not ever fitting in at school. The strength and grace of movement I lost with polio seemed to pale against the tenderness, beauty, and hope for acceptance that Cheryl represented to me. Even at twelve years of age, I understood how extraordinary and mysterious was the effect on my troubled spirit of Cheryl's simple, loving acceptance. As I dressed for school each day and as my vulnerable heart limped its way to Mr. Willbern's bus, all my thoughts were consumed with thoughts of her.

Throughout that sixth-grade year, on each and every one of our rides together, her smiles always met mine. My hurts were soothed and healed by her joy to be with me. Our conversations were simple and few. Yet, her words were not what healed me. It was her Divine presence.

Once sixth grade ended we both went to different schools and took other rides to school. Other than passing her house and seeing her in the yard or in a passing car, I rarely saw her.

Then fifteen years later, in the fall of 1975, I unexpectedly saw Cheryl at a University of Houston football sports banquet. I went with Mike "Crunchy" Johnston, a partner in the law firm where I worked. Mike had supported the Cougar defense as an All Southwest Conference linebacker from 1968 to 1971.

As I entered the cocktail reception area balancing a glass of merlot with my left hand and pushing the steering control on my motorized wheelchair with my right hand, I saw Cheryl standing in the middle of the crowd. She was with her boyfriend, Larry Keller, a former athlete at the University of Houston. Larry was on the active roster of the San Diego Chargers.

Even though she was a college senior, Cheryl gave me the same smile I had seen on that yellow school bus on the way to sixth grade. I rolled up to Cheryl and said," You look as pretty as the girl I remember being with every day on the bus going to Post Elementary School."

She introduced me to her boyfriend. She asked me how I had been. I thought for a second what it might have been like to be tall, muscular, and handsome, like Larry. Then, instantly I knew that if I had not had polio, I would never have had those bus rides with Cheryl. Those precious moments that had kept me going to a more sacred place in my life long after my days at Post Elementary School had ended. I wished Cheryl and her fiancé, Larry, well. Then, I joined my table to listen to the actor, Fred McMurray, give the main address.

Fred McMurray had been one of my heroes on television's *My Three Sons,* and those *Nutty Professor* and *Flubber* movies. As I shook Fred McMurray's hand that night, I told him that his acting and humor in the movies had worked powerful magic to draw my spirits out of darkness and depression after polio. However, seeing Cheryl that night reminded me that nothing drew my spirits out of darkness like Cheryl did by being herself on the sixth row of the bus. Those twenty minutes in the morning and in the afternoon on those school days were priceless, but also timeless and eternal. For a year, they were the only thing that seemed to matter.

A year or two after that fund-raising event at the University of Houston, my wife Dorothy and I drove down Emmott Road past Cheryl's childhood home. Turning right on Fairbanks-North Houston, we drove past the Airola home, where Batiste and Theresa Airola, Cheryl's maternal grandparents, lived and ran a dairy farm.

Dorothy and I drove past the same white farmhouse that I had frequented as a boy of four when my mother and I delivered home-baked chocolate chip cookies to Mrs. Airola and her nine-year old daughter, Margaret, who was already in an iron lung due to polio.

Suddenly, we saw a scene of shear mayhem. A passenger car with two occupants, a man and a woman, had been struck head-on by a station wagon. Paramedics were frantically trying to remove the woman from the front passenger seat. I commented to Dorothy at the time that I did not recognize any of the vehicles or persons at the scene. We drove on our way. I felt relieved that I did not know any of the persons involved in the accident.

The next day I learned that the woman had died. She had suffered a critical brain injury as a result of her head striking the door jamb at impact. Her life was taken by a drunk driver at the wheel of a station wagon. She was, indeed, someone I knew, after all. She was Cheryl Hagler.

I could not bear to attend the services. I did say prayers at home and at my church in thanksgiving for the gift from God that Cheryl was to me and those who knew her. I even wrote a poem honoring Cheryl and mailed it to her parents, Annie and Maynard Hagler. At the time and even now, that written homage to her memory seemed so insignificant compared to what I had received from Cheryl.

Over the years I have asked myself: *How do I let go of my grief for the loss of Cheryl? Why did God place her on the bus with me at that moment in my life?* I really never knew the answers to these questions, until now, as I sit writing this chapter.

On this day in January 2002, as I sit in my wheelchair writing this story, watching the crimson sun set over emerald blue-green Caribbean waters as glorious as the memories and difference Cheryl made for me, I close my eyes. Suddenly I am swept away to a place long ago but now as real and eternal as God's love for the both of us. I am a boy of twelve again. I smell my mother's cooking in my childhood home. With Charles, I rush out the door to catch the sixth-grade school bus. In all my awkwardness and embarrassment, I am helped on that bus. I look to the sixth-row seat with anticipation. There, Cheryl is smiling at me. I sit down next to her in the place of acceptance she has saved for me. We look into each other's eyes. She looks at me and sees an innocent and insecure child of God. I look into her face and see the face of an Angel on Earth. An Angel in Heaven, now.

My eyes open. As I continue writing about her, the sun sets on the horizon opposite the pure white sandy beaches. My pen stops writing at the end of the page describing nothing short of a miracle in my life. For all the incredible effect that she had on my heart, I never ever hugged Cheryl. I never ever kissed her, not even on the cheek. Now I wish I had. Sitting next to her I held her hand a time or two, risking a teasing from others on that bus. Yet, I am glad I did, especially today.

Darkness falls. The stars light up the sky. Finally, I give up to God my grief over the loss of Cheryl. I know that God saved a place for her in His Heavenly Kingdom as surely as His Angel saved a place for me each day on that bus. As the white-foam waves sound their washing away of the grieving sands of time, I pray, "God, thank You for sending me Your Angel Cheryl when I needed her the most."

God's message to me through Cheryl's existence on the bus is simple. Her presence invited me into the Divine. Perhaps, you feel the same invitation.

When you feel broken
When you feel hurt and alone
When taking the next breath
Or living another day
Seems an unbearable burden
Draw nearer to those who love you.
Look for an Angel on the bus
A stranger at Starbucks

A child of innocence at the store or on the beach
Or a person kneeling next to you at church.
Do you see an Angel bending over you?
Maybe, look at yourself in the mirror.
Perhaps God has chosen you
To be someone else's Angel.

I learned many things that sixth-grade year at Post Elementary School. However, the greatest lesson I learned was from you, dear Cheryl. I learned about angelic acceptance, about pure love and its amazing power to heal and keep on healing year after year.

CHAPTER 8

My Bending Angel of First Romantic Love

She stood by the windowpane
Crying like the rain,
From what I did not know.
For I could not reach her,
For what my love did not teach her,
Many years ago.

I have driven by her house countless times since the date we parted. Passing her home on the way to work, on the beautiful, meandering, pine-and-oak-canopied Memorial Drive, which starts at downtown Houston and makes its sleepy way to far west Houston, I always turn to glance at the French provincial-style house. I have reflected on the images of our relationship which began there in the spring of 1968 and ended there in the late winter of 1969.

In 1968, I had recovered as much as I could from the ravages of polio. In addition to the standard teenage pimples, and the uncomfortableness and awkwardness of being age

19, I carried a particular fear inside me—that the effects of polio left me unlovable and undesirable. Because of my mother's love and my faith in God, I felt as though I was enough of a person to offer and return love to a girlfriend and, maybe, a future wife. But, at that point, the reality of true love seemed unobtainable.

Although I had been fairly popular at Cy-Fair High School, I never had a relationship of mutual romantic love. In high school, when I called the girls I wished to date (sometimes, cheerleaders; other times, majorettes and beauty queens), "No" was the universal response. Following graduation in June of 1967, I went to Houston Baptist College in the fall. Then I transferred to the University of Houston the following spring. That same pattern of rejection continued. The coeds who did accept my invitation to go on a date seemed to say "yes" more out of obligation and kindness than out of a true desire to spend time with me. The ones who did go out with me, did it only once.

At that time, I was trying not to use my wheelchair very much. I wanted to be *normal*, whatever that meant. I wanted to walk and sit in normal chairs. I did my best to look normal and act normal when I was on a date. I knew deep down that I was not normal. Normality had ended with polio at age 6. A few girls made the best of it. However, I could tell each of the girls was very uncomfortable with me. Some seemed embarrassed and uncomfortable with how I appeared. Others seemed at a loss, not knowing what to do with me or for me.

They didn't know that I understood their confusion. After all, I had a two-inch riser on the bottom of my left shoe because my legs were different lengths. My hips tilted. My back was curved with scoliosis. My right arm was bent, deformed because of lack of triceps. My gait was far from balanced. When I took steps, my left leg stayed straight and my right foot nearly drug the ground. My right leg swung out to the right with every step. If I fell, I could not get up without assistance. It took great effort just to get out of the car and up on my feet to walk to the front door of my dates' homes. If I sat down in a chair or on a sofa, I needed assistance to get up. God forbid that I had to go to the bathroom and sit down on the commode. My date would be called upon to stand me up in the bathroom. More than once, I remember walking next to a date in college and in high school. She seemed to be embarrassed when others walking by us stared at me and looked at her. At moments like that I wanted to crawl under a rock.

Out of social desperation early in the spring semester of 1968, I called my cousin Melissa, a junior at Memorial High School. I asked Melissa if she could please, please, please fix me up with a blind date to go to an APO fraternity party at the University of Houston. Of my forty-five first cousins, Melissa has always been one of my favorites. She took chances and did for others. What she did for me this time led to the lips of an Angel. Finding Cindy was a direct result of Melissa doing such a caring, but risky thing for me and her—setting up a blind date. A blind date for me to see the beauty and wonder of God's Love.

Melissa said she would do what she could and call me back. The same day, she called me and said there was a classmate at Memorial High School who agreed to go to the fraternity party, sight unseen, with me. Melissa gave me her phone number and the address to pick her up. The day of the fraternity party, I was full of apprehension and anxiety. I shaved every whisker, washed and blew dried every hair, polished my shoes, brushed my teeth, and washed my parents' car, a Ford Galaxy 500. Full of anticipation, I made the twenty-minute drive to her home.

I turned left on Emmott Road, drove past the home of another Angel, Cheryl Hagler, took a right on Fairbanks North Houston, and passed the Ariola dairy. I thought about little nine-year old Margaret Ariola that I had seen in 1952 when I was four years old. Would polio cut off all my dreams of love as it had hers when she was confined to an iron lung? Left onto Hempstead Highway, a road I made weekday trips on to and from four hours of physical therapy from 1955 to 1958. Right onto Antoine. Left onto Old Katy Road. Now, right onto Silber Road. About a mile later my heart beat faster as I turned into the circle driveway of the house in which my blind date lived. What was about to happen? Would this be our first and last date? Would my date be embarrassed at the sight of me? Would she look at me and say, "This is a mistake. I cannot do this. I am so sorry."?

I remained committed. There was no turning back. I swung my car door out with my left knee. I lifted and dropped my left foot and leg out the door. With my left hand and arm, I pulled my right leg and foot out of the car and onto the pavement. To lower my center of gravity as much as possible, with my hands grasping the top of the door, I spread my legs as far apart as possible and rocked myself back and forth on stiff legs. With each rocking motion, my feet moved closer together until I stood straight up on two feet.

I walked to the front door and rang the bell. The door opened. An attractive woman said, "Hi. I am Aunt Ingrid. Please come in." She said that Cindy would be right down and I could wait for her in the living room. Aunt Ingrid did not stay to visit with me, but left the room instead. I sat down in a chair. A man came into the room and walked around a mirror-lined bar to mix a martini. He said, "Hello. I am Uncle Edward. I understand that you are a student at the University of Houston. What are you studying?"

"Political science," I replied.

Uncle Edward said, "Good subject," and then left the room.

I felt it odd that their reception for me was not longer and more welcoming. I thought that her aunt and uncle must have other things to do that were more pressing than getting to know me. A few minutes later, my date stepped down from the stairs. She smiled, said "Hello, Jack." She stepped toward me.

I looked at her and replied, "You look great. Are you ready to go?"

"Yes," she said.

Cindy could not have smiled more sweetly or more genuinely as she approached me as I sat in the living room chair. The way she looked at me—I knew instantly she was someone very special. I felt completely at ease in asking her if she would help me stand up. I held out my arms and hands in front of me as she extended her hands to grasp mine. I stiffened both legs as she pulled me upright toward her. I held her arm. She did not seem to mind. We walked out the front door. I walked around to the front of the car and opened the passenger door. She got in and I closed the door. I walked back around the car, got in, closed the door and turned the key.

As we drove to the APO fraternity party in Southampton near the UH campus, we chatted. She made me laugh. I made her laugh. At the fraternity party, we watched the UH Cougars play football on television. We visited with the fraternity brothers and sorority sisters. We had a wonderful time. I sat in a chair. Cindy sat on the floor in front of me. We drank cokes and ate Doritos. At the end of the evening, I drove slowly, winding my way back to her home on Memorial Drive. She could not have sat closer to me in the front seat of the car. I pulled the car up in the circle driveway once again. I was in a much different place than when we had met earlier that day. I had no fear anymore. I only had joyous expectations and true anticipation of what might come from this special relationship. I opened her door and walked her to the front door of the house. We looked into each other's eyes. I put my arms around her. Then, we shared the beauty of love's first sweet kiss.

For the next ten months, she and I were inseparable. Nearly every day after college classes, I drove to Memorial High School and picked up Cindy under the tall, slender pine trees on the north side of the school on Gaylord Street. Some days we sat for hours in the car and chatted. Other days we drove to the A&W on Westheimer Road and drank root beer. Almost every night at bedtime I called her or she called me to say goodnight. I counted on that daily routine, like sunrise or sunset. We could not wait to see each other the next day. I thought I had found my true love. We went to movies. We dined out. We played countless games of miniature golf at the Putt-Putt golf course, once located at Sage and Westheimer.

One evening my dear brother Charles, his date, Lynda, and Cindy and I played three rounds of Putt-Putt golf. Charles held my right upper arm to catch me if I fell. As I limped my way to the first tee, a group of teenage boys stared at me. They were sharing hurtful observations about me and laughing at me. Charles looked up at them and said, "You guys are real jerks." Cindy was offended too and did not distance herself from me in sharp contrast with the other girls when they were out with me in public.

We went to UH football games in the Astrodome. We fogged up car windows while kissing at drive-in movie theaters on cold Saturday nights. We went to Lake Livingston with friends and attended more football games and fraternity parties. We double-dated with my brother Charlie and his girlfriends. We went dancing to BYOB establishments, like the Club Royale and the Dixie Club on Dixie Drive, which catered almost exclusively to black clientele. We were not the least bit concerned with being two of the few white couples in the clubs to listen to the likes of Archie Bell and the Drells, and Otis Redding. I could not dance with her. Yet I found that I enjoyed watching her dance with my brother Charlie or with other patrons. Her moving to the Motown music made my heart dance in joy. Even in silence we enjoyed each other's company.

My polio did not ever seem to matter to her. Cindy's coming from a broken family did not concern me either. I had learned we had much in common by being different than others. Each of us had suffered brokenness; I with polio and her with separation from her immediate family. God uses that brokenness to bring people together, as Cindy and me, and invite Angels into their midst.

I did wonder what kind of hardships she must have suffered to not be living with her mother, father, or brother and instead be living with her aunt and uncle. I noticed that Cindy never said an unkind word about Uncle Edward and Aunt Ingrid. She must have felt very indebted to them for helping her at a time of great personal need. Not every family would take on raising a teenage girl, even one as sweet as she.

Cindy's acceptance of me was in sharp contrast to the way her aunt and uncle made me feel. Except for that first date when Aunt Ingrid greeted me at the front door and

Uncle Edward asked me what my major was, I never had another conversation with them about who I was, what mattered to me, or what I had accomplished in overcoming polio.

All went well between us until a February Sunday afternoon in 1969. I had stood with Cindy on the porch of my parents' home in Emmottville. As she stared out the window, she had tears in her eyes. The tears ran down her face too quickly to dry. She would not speak to me. She had seemed strangely quiet when I had picked her up earlier after church.

"Cindy, why are you crying?" I asked.

She didn't respond. We had always been able to talk about everything. Now she was unable to talk to me about anything.

I told her repeatedly that I loved her. I said, "My love is big enough to hear you say anything you need to say to me." That was of no comfort to Cindy as her tears continued to stream down her cheeks. After thirty minutes of tears and no explanation, in total exasperation I said," If you will not open up to me, I will take you home now."

She simply said, "Okay."

"Cindy, maybe we can talk tomorrow when you are not so upset," I replied in the hope that the chill of silence would be gone tomorrow.

I walked her to the car and tried to remain calm and strong. Surely, this day would not be the end of something as beautiful as us. She got in the car. I closed the door. I got in on the driver's side and looked at her. In tearful silence she sat as close to the passenger door as possible. What had I done or said? That twenty-minute drive to take her home seemed to take hours. I did not speak to her; she did not speak to me. We had spent hours upon hours enjoying our time together. This kind of silence was deafening. I pulled into the circle driveway. I said, "I hope you get to feeling better. I will call you later."

Cindy said nothing in reply. She just opened her door, got out, closed the door and walked stoically in front of the car and towards the front door of the house. Her face did not turn to look at me as she walked across the driveway. I waited in the car a few minutes, expecting her, as in the scene of a romantic movie, to run back into view, pull my door open, give me a hug and a kiss, and say she loved me. That did not happen. I started the car, and pulled forward to where I could see the front door of the home. It was closed.

Cindy was really gone.

I drove to my home as slowly as the speed limit allowed. I needed the time to contemplate what had just transpired. Honestly, I did not think that this was the ending of such a beautiful relationship. Such an ending seemed incomprehensible. I sought to convince myself that I just needed to give Cindy some space. I would go to college classes the next day and give her a call as usual. Maybe, she would be in a better place.

I sat in my classes the next day. I was physically present, but my mind was not really there. My spirit and heart were at that same special place and time on our first date when Cindy took my hands in hers as she stood me up in her living room. That place brought the remembrance of love's first kiss, of her love completing me and my love completing her.

At our respective ages of twenty and eighteen, admittedly romantic love is immature and complicated with layer upon layer of testosterone and estrogen. At this precarious time, I was not a boy nor was I yet a man, just as Cindy was not a girl nor was she yet a woman. I did not ever want to hurt her for I knew that with the separation from her family she must have been hurt enough. In our dating, I did not talk about my scars and wounds from polio. In turn, Cindy never said much about her own story, about the events that had taken place to cause her to live with an aunt and uncle instead of a mom, dad, and brother.

The next day after I got home from college, I set my books on my desk and called Cindy on the phone.

Her Aunt Ingrid answered, "Hello."

I asked, "May I please speak with Cindy?"

She paused for an uncomfortable eternity. She replied, "Let me see if she can come to the phone."

A few moments later Cindy picked up the phone. "Hello."

I said, "How are you?"

"Okay," she replied.

I asked, "Would like me to come over this evening after you have done your homework?" "No," she said.

I then said, "How about doing something this weekend?"

Cindy blurted out, "Jack, I cannot see you anymore."

I was stunned.

I sat in silence, in disbelief, at what I had just heard. It was such a stark contrast to everything leading up to the Sunday afternoon. As incomprehensible as this sounds, I did not plead with her to reconsider. I did not ask her what had happened. I sensed that her aunt and uncle did not approve of our relationship continuing. Had they forbidden Cindy from seeing me?

I felt sick and ill at ease, a little bit like the day I had called Cindy after my classes and her fourteen-year-old cousin Gina answered the phone. She said that Cindy was not at home. After a few minutes of small talk about her day at school, I asked her to have Cindy to call me. Later, the phone rang. It was Cindy. Without even a "hello", Cindy said that her Aunt Ingrid requested that under no circumstances was I ever to speak to Gina on the phone. I asked, "Why?" She said, "My Aunt Ingrid thinks it is very inappropriate for a college student like you to speak with a girl as young as Gina." That made me feel unwelcome, dirty, and ashamed.

I did not ask Cindy for confirmation that her aunt and uncle had ordered her not to see me any longer. The last thing I wanted to do was to try to save our relationship by attacking or confronting the same people who had supported her at a time of great need. I also did not want to hurt her for she had been hurt enough.

A voice within me said, "Jack, if you really love Cindy, you need to let her go. If your love for each other is true, in time it will work out if it is meant to be". So, to her words "I cannot see you anymore" all I said was, "Okay. Goodbye."

Then it was my turn to cry.

As the red buds and plum trees were blooming, as the green herons were precariously building their nests in the tops of the pine trees, as the daffodils were flowering yellow and white, and as the white oak trees were raining the pollen and seeds of new growth on our heads, our relationship had died. Spring was at hand, but our love was frozen in the grasp of despair, like that on Good Friday.

Our love ended as mysteriously as it had begun. Cindy came into my life suddenly and unexpectedly and brought me great joy and peace. Just as suddenly and unexpectedly, she left. Although that was the immediate end, it was never the real ending of our relationship for me. God brought her into my life at that moment and time for a purpose. Hopefully, in some way I did as much for her as she did for me back then, since then, and even now.

As I drive by her house one last time before I finish

writing the last page of this chapter, I see that a wrought iron and brick fence has been erected which separates the French provincial home from the street view. The lapse of forty-five years and the construction of a brick and wrought iron fence do not obstruct my ability to see today what God created as a blessing for me.

It is April of 1968. From Memorial Drive, I see a nineteen-year-old polio survivor getting out of a Ford Galaxy 500. He is there to pick up his girlfriend. They are going to see *Planet of the Apes*, starring actor Charlton Heston at the Garden Oaks Theater. The young man with long side burns and a smile on his face walks with a limp to the front door. The door opens. There she is. He glances at her feet and notices black leather shoes. She is wearing a beautiful, blue satiny-silk dress, the hem of which touches the mid-point of her knees. A lightweight, dark navy wool sweater wraps around her shoulders. He sees her dark, thick, shiny hair which flips up and curls at the base of her neck. He steps closer. He sees her soft white skin and her rosy lips. The sweetness of her perfume is only exceeded by the aroma of the magnolia blossom she has taken from her uncle's tree in the backyard and placed in her hair above her left ear. He looks at her face. He sees a wonderful smile, full of joy for another evening together. He puts his arms around her. She places her arms around him. They share love's sweet kiss. She looks at him with her beautiful eyes.

He thinks for a minute she is looking at him the way that an Angel looks at all of God's children. She does not see a handicapped, disabled, or broken person. Rather, she sees a child complete in the Eyes of God. Because of her as God's Bending Angel, he feels that his gait is normal. His legs and arms are even and symmetrical. His spine is no longer curved. He is much taller, not with stunted growth because of polio. His back is straight. His muscles are strong. The scars on his hands, his thumbs, his wrists, his right upper leg, the scars from the base of his neck and down his back to his tailbone, and on his feet, disappear. He no longer has polio. He is as healthy, as lovable, and loved as the boy he was before polio. He is not cured because of God's love through her. He is healed.

Over the last forty-five years, I have wondered many times why my Bending Angel of teenage love said she could not see me anymore. Didn't I mean to her what she meant to me? Did she just stop loving me? Had she found someone else? Had I done or said something so wrong or hurtful to her that I was to blame for losing her? What about me, if anything, caused her Aunt and Uncle to forbid her from seeing me again? Did she ever think of me as an instrument of God's love to her like I thought of her? What has her life been like since our parting?

In the end, those questions are not important in the story of my teenage Bending Angel. What truly matters is what happened then between us.

Our relationship officially ended over forty-five years ago. But, for me, it never really ended. I give thanks to God for the message He gave me and for Cindy, His messenger. Through her as my Bending Angel, I received a gift that has never died. Her loving embrace held for me God's unmistakable promise that I would one day find my true love and my true love would find me.

On the first day we met in 1968 and on the final day of our parting, I believe there was another Angel standing watch over us. Did that Angel lead us to one another? As I write this last page of this chapter in the book of my life, did that same Angel beckon me to drive by this place again and to see what God witnessed between Cindy and me so long ago?

Indeed the driveway is now transected by a brick wall and an iron gate. Yet the circle of love which began and ended there with Cindy was never really broken. For that circle of love and my teenage Bending Angel both led me to my one true love, Dorothy. Just three years later I became Dorothy's groom and Cindy became someone else's bride.

In the sudden and unexpected ending of this our relationship, I never had the chance to say goodbye to Cindy. That sunny but chilly Sunday afternoon when she exited my car, I had no chance to give her one last embrace. There was no farewell kiss.

I never called Cindy or wrote her a letter to thank her. This chapter is my way of finally saying thanks to her and to God for her acts of love as one of God's Angels bending over me.

I complete my last stroke of the pen. The ink has dried on the paper. I finally turn this page in the book of my life. To God, I give thanks and praise for all you did and all you are, Cindy, my Bending Angel of Teenage Love. Did another Angel see the two of us from above? Did the Angel see what we could both become with God's Love?

Auntie reunion caricature

Jack and Auntie

Carolyn and Jack with Old Donk, 1951

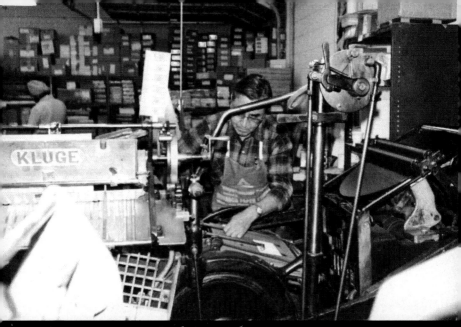

Coach Oscar Ochoa, Pressman

Jack and cousin Bobby, 1958

Jack, 1958

Charles and Jack after church, April 1958

Angel Cheryl before her tragic death

Angel Cheryl Hagler as seen on Jack's School Bus

Jack proposed to Dorothy, January 1972   *Jack and Dorothy cruising, 1996*

Dorothy, Jack and Grandmother Jennie Emmott, 1972

*Charles first grade at
Ridgecrest Elementary*

*Charles and Dad displaying catch at
Chandeleur Islands, LA 1978*

Jack and Charles - Best Man, May 20, 1972

Russell, Rev. Cal Rutherford, Rev. Richard Wheatcroft, Gary, Dorothy and Jack

Charles and Jack joint birthday, August 1954

Russell, Charles, Carolyn, Jack and Gary, spring 1965

Dad and Mom in front of first home, 1946

Mom, Dad and Carolyn, 1947

Jack in his bassinette in the upstairs bedroom, fall 1948

Carolyn, Charles, Jack after church, 1952

Mom and Jack, fall 1948

Jack after polio 1955

CHAPTER 9

The Angel Who Opens Doors

In life and love, many doors are closed for each of us. Yet, God's love for us asks us to bravely step over the threshold of the present and into the unfamiliar place where our dreams await us.

I believe God sent an Angel to open a door for me. That door led to attending law school and becoming a lawyer, my truest vocation. That door also opened a pathway for another precious dream of mine to come true.

I had met Ron Trull first when I was a senior at Cy-Fair High School. He worked as a rehabilitation counselor for the Texas Rehabilitation Commission (TRC) to provide public assistance to students with disabilities who had work potential. Ron knew that education and training were the keys to finding and keeping a job and earning a living. That was even more important for the disabled since the vast majority of disabled persons in America were, and are, unemployed.

I transferred to the University of Houston in the spring

of 1968 after one semester at Houston Baptist College. The TRC supported me at UH by paying for my tuition, books, and fees. I was not a model student for my first two years at UH. I even joked with my friends that I majored in "Playing Bridge" at the Cougar Den. I skipped classes to play bridge with my friends; when I needed to study, I played bridge. I took my exams, but my test scores finally made Ron question whether I was really a college-worthy student.

By the fall of 1970, my grades were so deplorable that I was placed on academic probation. Ron called me into his office and sat me down. He said, "Jack, this is the last semester that the TRC will support your education. Financial resources are always under attack as something to be cut in governmental programs." He then added, "The TRC supports students who make proper use of the opportunity to learn."

I left Ron's office embarrassed and disgusted at my mediocre effort. You might say this was a real wakeup call. At about this same time, I met an unusually wonderful sweet and supportive young woman by the name of Dorothy Lansford at a religious retreat at St. Francis Episcopal Church. It was no coincidence that Ron Trull, Dorothy and I crossed paths at this time. Sometimes it takes more than one Angel to deliver a message and to make a difference, to support a person in accomplishing dreams and overcoming adversity.

Soon after the retreat I stopped attending bridge-playing "classes" in the Cougar Den. Instead, I attended all my scheduled classes and took all of my exams. Dorothy helped type my papers. She also provided a quiet place for my studies and exam preparation at her apartment.

My grades went from poor to excellent. The kernel of my unspoken dream to become a lawyer grew inside of me, now that I had a reliable study schedule and could find quiet time to think deeply about my future, now that Dorothy was in my presence.

I studied very hard for the LSAT, the Law School Aptitude Test. I did not have the opportunity to take an LSAT for people with disabilities. There were no time adjustments for my lack of speed in writing. As a result, my LSAT score was terrible.

Even though I completed my Bachelor of Arts in December of 1971, I couldn't apply for law school until the spring of 1972. So, I took a part-time substitute teaching position with the Cy-Fair district making a glorious $20 per day.

That same fall Dorothy and I had gone up to the University of Texas and taken a self-guided tour of the law school. I'd picked up the application forms and met the Dean of Students, T.J. Gibson.

When Dorothy and I met with T.J., I told him about my stellar grades in the second half of undergraduate school and my poor test results for the LSAT. He said it was very competitive to get into UT because the best and brightest graduates from all over the country would be applying. Only one in twenty applicants would be accepted. He did say, however, that the Admissions Committee had the power to make exceptions. He encouraged me to apply and see what happened. He made no promises.

As Dorothy wheeled me through the halls of the UT law school, I felt that it was a place where I belonged, where I was destined to be. It felt comfortable, like an old pair of jeans or the blue Madras plaid shirt from high school that kept getting softer and softer with each washing. After all, my dad had attended UT and played intramural basketball for them in the early 1940s. He had met my mother there and fallen in love with her just blocks from where we were now.

My feelings of destiny flew in the face of reality. With polio, I knew that dreams don't always come true. Some dreams die a slow, painful death while others vaporize in an instant. I felt badly that a lack of dedication in my early college years might cost me my dream. That had nothing to do with polio. That part was my failed sense of responsibility.

I applied to most of the other law schools in Texas. I even applied to Harvard Law School. For the $50 application fee there, I got a beautiful certificate, suitable for framing, denying my admission.

With Dorothy's help, I completed the UT application. I obtained letters of recommendation, references and my transcript. My parents' friend, Bud Campbell, V.P. of Tenneco, and Leroy Jeffers, then President of the State Bar of Texas, wrote letters of recommendation. I wrote a letter to the UT Admissions Committee explaining why I wanted to be a lawyer and why I deserved to be admitted. Then, the long wait began.

My daily routine was to complete my teaching assignment. Go home. Then I waited for the mail to arrive. Most days there would be nothing in the mail for me. Just bills and mail for my parents. One day, I did receive an envelope from the University of Texas School of Law. It was very thin.

I said a prayer before opening the envelope, "God, please let this be a notice of admission."

Isn't it true that we humans are very good about asking God for what we want?

It read, "Dear Mr. Emmott. We regret to inform you that..."

I was crushed.

The next day I called Ron to tell him that I had been

declined for admission. I then called T.J. Gibson to see if there was an appeals process. T.J. said that there was a process and that the law school admission board would soon be meeting to consider appeals. He told me to write a letter to the law school admissions committee asking that my application be reconsidered.

A couple of weeks later, Dorothy and I took that letter to T.J.'s office on the morning of the day that the admissions committee was to hear my appeal. I told him how important it was that my appeal be granted. I promised to work very hard to become a very good student and lawyer.

T.J. said he would present my case to the admissions committee and call me later that day. I decided to have an all-day vigil at the apartment of my cousin Bob in Austin.

Late in the afternoon, the phone rang. It was T.J. There was hesitation in his voice. TJ said, "Jack, your appeal came very close to being granted. There were those on the committee who wanted you to be given a chance, and others who said your objective test results and grade scores did not warrant your admission and the refusal to admit other applicants who were more qualified. In the end, those who considered objective data won out."

I had lost. Our vigil turned into a wake instead of a celebration.

Later that day, instead of driving the most direct route on Interstate 35 from Bobby's apartment to Highway 290, I drove past the UT football stadium and up the hill towards the law school building. I stopped in front of Townes Hall. I looked up the hill at the imposing stone edifice of the law school building. I couldn't believe it would not be my home to obtain a law degree. I looked into Dorothy's eyes, "I am so afraid I will not go to law school here. I feel so strongly that this is the place where I belong. I must find a way to keep alive this hope to learn here. If not, I do not know what I will do in my life. All of my other applications were rejected, too."

The next day in Houston, I called Ron. I told him that I was afraid that I would never get a law degree, and that Austin and UT would not be my home. I remember saying: "Ron, all I want is a chance to succeed, even if I fail. I know with dedication and hard work I can make it through law school if I am given the chance," I said.

Ron said, "I will do anything I can do help. What do you want me to do?"

I replied, "Would you go up and meet personally with T.J. Gibson and ask that I be given a second appeal?"

Ron replied, "Yes."

For cathartic reasons, I began to write another letter to the UT Law School Admissions Committee. The letter was an outpouring of emotion, not intended to be shared. A few days later, I called Ron, "Could I go with you to Austin when you meet with T.J.?"

Ron replied, "Yes, but it would be better if it was just me as a representative of the TRC meeting alone with T.J. Gibson."

The next week Ron called. "I have a meeting with Dean Gibson. Do you still want to go?"

"Yes," I replied. "I will stay at my Cousin Bob's apartment while you meet with the Dean."

The next day, Ron picked me up in his Volkswagen Beetle for the drive to Austin on that sunny spring day. I did not notice the bluebonnets or Indian paint brushes. I was absorbed in reading my cathartic letter to Ron. (That letter is in a box somewhere in my attic.) I vividly recall the theme of the letter.

"Ron," I said. "God wants all of his flock to have a chance

to succeed or to fail. I have suffered twice with being declined for admission and then my appeal being denied. With God, you and T.J., I feel there is still hope to resurrect my chances of attending UT law school. After all, God is all about second chances.

"For me, it is about overcoming adversity. It is about having faith that light lies ahead of the darkness. If every child of God like me is good enough for God, why cannot I be good enough to get that chance, that opportunity to become the law student and lawyer of my dreams?"

That letter traced my suffering with polio, my rehabilitation, my surgeries and my education. I asked him: "Ron, didn't overcoming such things matter to people on the admission committee? What about the human potential inside me? Doesn't it matter more than test scores and GPAs? America is made up of people who are objectively average in intellect but do extraordinary things."

Ron listened to my one-way conversation and as we neared the city limits of Austin, I asked Ron, "Do you believe in God?"

He hesitated. He seemed uncomfortable with the question. "Jack, I do not believe in God. Right now, I do not know whether I am an atheist or an agnostic."

I replied, "But Ron, without faith in God, what is important in life, love and death? What is the purpose of our births or deaths?"

He didn't have a reply.

Ron dropped me off at Bobby's apartment. He drove to the law school. Then he went to meet with T.J. Two hours later, Ron picked me up from the apartment. He was very quiet as we drove Highway 290 East back to Houston.

I broke the silence and said, "Well, Ron, tell me how did it go?"

Ron said, "I don't really know. Dean Gibson listened to me. I could tell he really wants you to be admitted."

At one point near the end of the meeting, Ron said Dean Gibson opened up a file drawer next to his desk. He brushed his fingers past the open files and said, "Look. Here are over two thousand applications for admission. It is very competitive to get admitted to the law school in this environment."

At that point, Ron opened up his brief case and pulled out a piece of paper. It was an itemized statement of all monies that the TRC had spent on my undergraduate education and rehabilitation. Ron said to Dean Gibson, "This is all of the money the State of Texas has invested in this young man. For this investment of tax dollars to pay off, Jack needs an education. Will you tell the admissions committee that the only way this investment has a chance to pay off is for Jack to be admitted? If Jack fails, so be it, but he deserves a chance to become a lawyer and to be a tax-paying citizen." (Statistics had shown at that time that every dollar invested by the TRC in education and vocational rehabilitation is paid back to the State by the recipient many times over in taxes during his or her career.)

"I will let the committee know this and send Jack a letter as to the second appeal process," replied Dean Gibson.

Back home, for the next few weeks, the routine was the same when I returned home from teaching. When would the letter come? When would the letter come? After a few weeks, I gave up hope. I stopped going to the mail box. I left it up to my brother Gary to bring home the mail each day and let me know if there was an envelope from UT. "No, Bubba. Nothing from UT today," was his daily report.

Then, on a day I had not asked my brother Gary about the mail, I sat alone in the dark after dinner in my parents' house. I shuffled through the day's mail. I saw a big, fat letter-size envelope from the University of Texas School of Law. My heart started pounding. I called Dorothy on the phone. "Dorothy, Gary picked up the mail today. He did not tell me I had a letter from UT Law School. Will you stay on the phone as I open the envelope?"

"Yes, of course," she said.

I tore the envelope open. "We are pleased to inform you that you have been admitted for the class commencing June 1972." I started screaming for my parents who were upstairs in their bedroom. Mom ran down the stairs thinking that something terrible must have happened. To her delight, she read the letter and started screaming herself, "Come down here, Jack! Come down here!" Dad ran down the stairs in his white boxer underwear and sleeveless T-shirt and was wondering what all the pandemonium was about. Mother and I told him. We all had tears of joy in our eyes.

I borrowed the car from mother. I stopped to buy some cheap Annie Green Springs wine as I drove over to Dorothy's apartment to celebrate. It was after 11:00 p.m. After a few sips of wine, I called Ron. "Ron, sorry I am calling you so late this evening. I got a letter of acceptance to UT Law School today! I start classes in June!"

Ron erupted with laughter.

"Ron, thanks for going to bat for me at UT, to care enough to be there for me."

Not everyone takes the time to stick out his neck for others. Ron had done that for me. He opened his wings of hope for me and a big door to my future.

The next day, I called Ron at work to see how his day was going. Ron said, "I wrote on the chalk board in my office, We Made It! UT All The Way!"

Since I graduated from law school in August of 1974, Ron and I had periodically spoken about those moments of rejection and acceptance we lived through together.

In the 1980s, he had me come to Austin to speak about my experience at a conference for rehab counselors at the TRC building. I can still see the radiance of Ron's smile and his beaming eyes as he listened to my talk. For my success was really a reflection of who he was and what he did, and the part he took in opening a door to making a dream come true for me.

In the summer of 2010, it had been a few years since I had touched base with Ron. I tried to call my old phone numbers for him. They no longer worked. I assumed by now he had retired. He had told me he dreamed of owning a home in Bastrop, Texas.

When I was trying to reach him, I wanted to express again my gratitude for him being the Angel who opened that door for me at such a critical time in my quest for a legal education. When I could not find Ron's number, I decided to Google him. His name came up on the first page of my search, "Ron Trull died February 22, 2010, Bastrop, Texas." The beautifully written obituary published in *Bastrop Examiner* set forth the story of Ron's life, and his commitment to his family and service to God. You see, years after our chat about faith and belief in God, Ron found his own way back to a life of faith.

Ron had indeed purchased that retirement home in Bastrop and was a church leader at the First Baptist Church of Bastrop, Texas. I read the blog Ron had started to talk about his journey towards recovery and possible death from spinal cancer.

I always wanted to do something great for Ron that could measure up to what he had done for me. When my law school application was accepted, I said, "Ron, if I ever get to be Governor, I intend to appoint you to serve as the

Commissioner for the TRC. Texas needs someone like you to serve in that capacity."

I feel badly that dream never came to pass. Ron's smile at me when I said that to him through the years let me know that he understood my gratitude.

I guess that the greatest thing that I did for Ron was to step over the threshold of the door he opened for me and seize the dream that God wished for me.

Despite his strong Christian faith, medical care, and supportive and beautiful wife, Judy, and family, there were no more "appeals" for Ron, like mine, following his unsuccessful treatment for cancer. Unlike the letter of acceptance I got from UT, the door to recovery slammed shut for him.

However, the Risen Christ opened the Gates of Heaven for Ron just as Ron opened that door for him like he opened the door for me at UT. One day he will greet me at our Father's Home. I will have the opportunity to thank him for what he did for me. An Angel. A door. A dream.

CHAPTER 10

Dorothy, the Angel of True Love

I was not looking for this next Angel. She now says she was not looking for me.

I believe all love stories are created by God. God sends to each of us a Holy Messenger of true love. Our role is to find that true love just as we are called by God to find and follow our faith in His Son, the Risen Christ. If our hearts meet at the crossroads of Heaven and Earth, God wants us to cling to one another and to that Holy Gift of Divine Love. That Love is the reason such Holy Messengers lead us into the sacrament of marriage. A union. A blessed relationship in which the seemingly impossible becomes possible. In the flowering of that Love, miracles are experienced as wondrously as when Christ turned water into wine at Canaan.

I believe that this story of Dorothy and our true love began long before my birth. Could it have been that the genesis of our love began like this?

One day in God's time, a precious spirit, an Angel in Heaven, heard the voice of God. "You, my dear Angel, have to leave me for a while."

The Angel replied, "I do not want to leave you, my Father. Here in the presence of Your Holy Grace, I am at peace. My heart overflows with joy."

God responded, "All those who are the product of my Love, including you, are created for my own Divine purpose. The time has come for you to fulfill your purpose, to be my messenger, one of my Bending Angels on Earth. Please kneel before me, your God. Now, I must remove your wings. You cannot take them with you. You must leave them with me."

The Angel anxiously said, "But, Father, if you take my wings, I will no longer be an Angel!"

God exclaimed, "My dear, wings are not what make you an Angel. The works you do in My Name, how your acts reflect My Love and how your deeds shine will be angelic.

"When you have finished on Earth, and served me well, I will send an Angel to pin your perfect wings back on you. You will be commanded to kneel and to bend over again. Then your wings will be re-attached."

"But why must I go?" the Angel asked.

"There is a special boy, an innocent child, who will have polio. The reason I created him cannot be fulfilled without you. In helping him know Me, you will allow the boy to find true love and the Angel in you. In a way you do not yet understand, you will come to know that this boy and his love will become another of my blessings to you.

"Now, I bless you and send you on your way. When you open your eyes on Earth as one of my newborn children, you will see the guardian Angel I have selected for you. You will call her 'Mother.' Amen."

* * *

I had resisted a strong temptation to sleep in on a Saturday morning and reluctantly came to a retreat named *The Narrow Ridge* at St. Francis Episcopal Church, my lifelong parish.

On this January day in 1971, the Director of Christian Education, Marilyn Black, had invited me to attend this one-day spiritual retreat. Marilyn said she would be watching for me to pull up in my car so that when I arrived she could send someone to pull my wheelchair out of the backseat and help me get out of the front seat and into the chair. The person who Marilyn (and God) sent me was a young woman I'd never met named Dorothy Lansford.

I remember noticing a certain sweetness and kindness in her face as she walked to the car. Dorothy eagerly and carefully helped me into the wheelchair. She pushed me into the Guild Room in which twenty other people were seated. During the day we learned that "The Narrow Ridge" was the path we needed to travel in our walk of faith. We explored what that path required of us, and what the consequences were if we did not stay on a Holy path, but fell off the ridge and into sin separating us from one another and our God.

Dorothy sat next to me, on my right. She made sure I was comfortable all day by asking considerate questions and by her graceful, small gestures.

"Jack, can I get you something to drink?"

"Would you care for a donut? Please let me know if can help you in any way so that you may better enjoy the retreat."

I learned she taught Sunday school classes under Marilyn's supervision. She was from Port Lavaca and a legal secretary. Her mother and sister were also members of the Church.

At noon it was time for our lunch break. We had the typical church buffet: spaghetti with meat sauce, Caesar salad, sourdough bread with butter and iced tea. The sweet ladies of the church had provided cake and cookies for dessert. I did not know how Dorothy felt about me as we both sat down at the lunch table. For me, there was no spark, no blast of affection, and certainly no "love at first sight."

I noticed that I enjoyed Dorothy's company. Her mere presence was a comfort. As we sat across from each other at the table, an elderly woman approached us. She wore an elegant hat, hose and high heels, and a mink stole which smelled like mothballs. Standing next to us with her plate of food she asked, "Could I please sit down with you and have lunch?" I thought to myself, *Yes, please join us, but could you leave the pungent mothballs outside the door?* Instead, I took a difficult mothball-filled breath and choked out my response, "Yes, please do join us. That would be nice." After a couple of minutes, the lady looked at us and to my complete surprise, said, "You are such a cute couple. How long have you been married?" I thought to myself how bizarre. How could this woman think we were a married couple? Dorothy and I had just met.

I never saw that woman again, at church or otherwise. She did not attend the retreat. I have often wondered if she might have been an Angel in disguise. Did God send her to our table to give me a glimpse of what was in store for us? Was she, the "Mothball Angel," sent to shock my senses and to declare: "Be watchful. You never know when you are in the presence of Divine Love."?

Following the retreat, Dorothy and I started dating. Sometimes we went to movies. Dorothy spent many days and evenings in Emmottville, my childhood home. The greatest gift for me was that I could be who I was when I was with her. I was attracted to Dorothy because of her deep inviting brown eyes, smiling face, indelible sweetness and heartfelt caring. I was also very much drawn to what she did not have. She did *not* have an air of pretension. She did *not* try to fake a personality. She did *not* place a curtain of changeable moods or prickly petulance between us. The beauty and strong, honest heart within her was there to be seen, to be appreciated and cherished.

In addition to these genuine gifts of soul, there had been situations requiring tensile character strength that Dorothy had dealt with already. For instance, she did not have a traditional two-parent family. Her father had been absent for most of the years when a father could have offered stability and nurturing. She only had her sweet and dear mother named Ellen.

Behind her infectious laughter and her cheerful personality, I sensed a void left by the failures of Dorothy's dad to truly "father" his child. There was something in that absence, that imperfection of circumstance that I felt drawn to. Could I step into that absence and be used as an instrument of God's love to help Dorothy experience, as an adult, the care and steadying love she had missed as a child due to her absent father?

Later I discovered inside that void an Angel of God was sent to me. An Angel who graced me then and thereafter with a bountiful, unconditional love which completed me, just as I hoped one day my love might help complete Dorothy to make up some of what she had lost. In that inviting space stood an Angel bending over me to make up for and to heal what I too had lost and my obvious lack of muscular strength, straight bones and unscarred flesh. Through Dorothy's presence I was learning how to become a part of something much bigger than myself, how to become a true partner in a long term romantic relationship.

On the practical side, Dorothy was game for anything I wanted to do. My nature was to be in constant motion. In contrast, Dorothy was just as happy with a cup of coffee in one hand and a good book to read in the other. She never complained, though. She did work her magic by helping me find a better balance between activity and rest. In an inexplicable way she enabled me to focus on what was most important: to be nearer to God and to honor the opportunities to grow, to learn, to achieve and to love.

In yielding to my desire to go places, I sometimes accidentally put her in an awkward position. On one such occasion we went fishing at Lake Houston at Uncle Army's and Aunt Sarah's cedar cabin on Moonshine Hill Road in Humble, Texas.

We drove our car out to Old Humble Road. About the point of the Artesian Well in Old Town Humble, there was a bait camp. In the darkness one morning at six a.m., I parked the car in front of the bait store, and said, "Dorothy, would you please go in and buy some minnows, hooks and weights?" I gave her the money. Since it was a hassle for her to get the wheelchair out, put me in it, and roll me into the bait camp, I thought it was only logical to have her go inside without me. Easier for me; easier for her. As I sat outside the bait camp, I saw Dorothy's head pop out the door. "Jack, do you want small, medium or large minnows? They have all three." I replied, "Medium." Then Dorothy disappeared for a few more minutes and her head popped out the door again. "Jack, do you want small, medium or large hooks?" I replied, "Medium." There were other customers in the bait camp. The proprietor was growing very impatient with a lazy man sitting in a car behind the wheel in the parking lot sending a woman in to do what was clearly a man's job. He could not understand why I did not just come inside and handle this. Then, it came to the weights Dorothy needed to buy. The proprietor had a very large selection of weights. He knew what was coming next. When Dorothy opened the door to yell out the weight choices, the proprietor looked at Dorothy and exasperatedly said, "What's wrong with your husband? Why can't he come in here? Is he crippled or something?" Dorothy paused and said, "He is not my husband, but he is crippled." The owner of the bait camp felt so bad he quickly gave her the minnows, hooks and weights without charge and said, "I am so sorry. Please do come back anytime."

The other thing I noticed about Dorothy was that the more time I spent with her, the better I became. I was happier, more secure, and healthier. My college grades went from poor to excellent. In my last two years at UH, I met Dorothy after my classes. I studied late at night at her apartment, sometimes while she slept. Occasionally I fell asleep being too tired to drive home. The next morning, as I rushed to leave, Dorothy always got up and insisted on cooking me breakfast before I left. She would open the windows. Watching her cook by the stove and feeling the breeze moving through the dining room are things I treasure to this day. At such times I had the comfort of not having a care or worry in the world.

On many occasions Dorothy stayed up late at night and typed papers for me after she had worked all day as a legal secretary at a nationally known bankruptcy law firm. Who was this person who cared for me with such devotion?

I began teaching Sunday school classes as Dorothy already did. Teaching God's Word brought me unexpected joy and pride. Meeting with the other teachers on Wednesday nights in the same room where I had practiced at ages five and seven in the Cherub Choir brought back acute memories of feeling so much a part of something special, something bigger than me and something Divine that I so believed in. The red and white robe with the large red bowtie whose flowing ends lay across my small chest as I sang my favorite hymn " Jesus Loves Me, This I Know" were the outward manifestations of my heart-swelling love of God and His unshakeable Love for me and all creation.

Dorothy and I developed a Friday night ritual. We would go to Weingarten's grocery store and buy a bottle of Annie Green Springs blueberry wine, two rib-eye steaks, tater tots, asparagus, apple turnovers, and Blue Bell vanilla ice cream. We would then consume the feast. We celebrated each of our successes the prior week. Then, we kissed and embraced each other before I left to return to home in Emmottville.

As our relationship took shape, it became increasingly important to me to not ever be in a position of breaking her heart—her father had already done enough of that. I also did not want to be a bother or a burden. From the very beginning, I had sensed that Dorothy loved me. She said, "I love you," long before I could. I was not going to give my heart permission in rest, playfulness, or heady passion to say to her "I love you" when I was not certain ours was the one, true, everlasting love of my life.

It was becoming increasingly uncomfortable not to echo Dorothy's words of love. But even more uncomfortable would have been my professing love without my love for her being as true and deep as I knew she deserved. I started reading the works of Khalil Gibran to Dorothy. Gibran's descriptions of love helped me as I wrestled with whether I had found my true love and if my true love had found me. In reality, my journey through the darkness of Advent to the birth of the Christ Child and the Light of Christmas Day echoed my journey toward the truth buried inside my heart toward Dorothy.

I knew I needed to sit down in the quiet at my desk and write down the reasons why I loved Dorothy enough to say: "I love you. Will you marry me?", or write her a letter of heartbreak and good-bye.

I started thinking about my immature picture at the age of 18 of an ideal wife I had conceived long before I met Dorothy. A Hugh Hefner Playboy Bunny with air-brushed, perfect skin from a well-connected wealthy family. I realized that prior to meeting me Dorothy must have had her own thoughts of an "ideal husband"—one who could dress and care for himself, dance with her, look normal and be strong enough to carry her in his arms over the threshold after the wedding. What better example was there of a lack of completeness, normality and self-reliance than me? What kind of exquisite love did Dorothy have which had already accepted me as her one-and-only? Why did my imperfections not matter to her? Why was she blind to me being lame?

I sat down to pen the logical reasons why I could or could not give my heart permission to love Dorothy. It was as if my hand was paralyzed again by polio's onset at age six. I was not able to write on paper the reasons which had held back my heart for so long. Those "logical" thoughts had almost totally eclipsed the truer, deeper feelings of love I held in my heart for her. As I held the pen above the paper, I closed my eyes in prayer. "God, what shall I do?"

In the darkness, I saw the light of Dorothy's sweet beautiful face looking at me. In that moment I knew we were meant to be friends and lovers forever. The cold thoughts of saying good-bye were thwarted by warm tears, which ran down my cheeks and onto the paper.

At that moment of Epiphany, I heard the Heavenly Voice

of an Angel say to me: "Jack, she is the one. Let go of reason. Follow your heart. Open your eyes. See her as the Angel that God has sent to save you from yourself. Give to her your broken, frail, vulnerable parts. You will be made whole, completed in her love. She will see her own Angel in you. You are both loved by God."

The words of this Angel were louder, truer, and deeper than my doubts and fears.

This unlikely, unexpected one, my beautiful Dorothy with long blond hair and dark brown smiling eyes not only became my best friend and lover. She became a Holy instrument to let me see, know and experience the depth of God's love for me.

Dorothy means "Gift from God." At age twenty-two, I knew when I met Dorothy she was special. I did not know she was, in fact, God's special gift to me. Equally important, I did not know whether I might become that same gift for her. She did not have a real father. She had an extraordinary mother with lupus, a sister with lupus, and a Vietnam veteran brother with diabetes and Agent Orange disease. I found that both our love for each other and God's love for us were big and full enough to joyfully accept our part in caring for them and them for us. Dorothy did not have monetary wealth. She did have a far greater treasure in her love for me. All of me. The broken parts in need of healing. The naked, vulnerable, ugly, deformed, scarred and painfully hard-to-see parts of my body that were visible to her eyes when we made love after our marriage or when she dressed or bathed me.

At that moment of overflowing tears I knew I could say "I love you" to Dorothy and really mean it. When I said "I love you" to Dorothy, it would also mean "Will you marry me?"

I gave great thought to selecting a place to make my proposal of marriage to Dorothy. It did not need to be a fancy restaurant or a romantic far-off getaway because the location of our love was sacred. It traveled wherever we were. But I wanted it to be a place we would both remember fondly for the rest of our lives.

In 1972, on a beautiful January spring-like afternoon, I decided to take Dorothy to Uncle Army's and Aunt Sarah's cabin on Moonshine Hill Road. I could not get down on my knees; I could ask Dorothy to go fishing with me. As we sat next to each other on the pier with the birds singing and Uncle Army riding the lawn tractor in the yard, I said to Dorothy, "I love you. Will you marry me?" "Yes," she replied. The promise and hope of true love and marriage was sealed with a kiss.

I had had many thoughts about what it would mean to be a husband to Dorothy and a father to children. A father who did not let her or the kids down. A husband who would always be around. I wanted our children to have a father they could be proud of. With her at my side, I wanted to show the world what is possible with love and what can be overcome with healing and Godly Grace.

On May 20, 1972, we were married at St. Francis. Contrasted to the destination weddings of today and the huge dollars that are spent to make such occasions exquisitely memorable, beautiful, delicious and extraordinary, our wedding holds a candle to any wedding I have attended since that date. It was a wedding put on by a "village" of our family and friends. We wrote our own vows, used music we had chosen, and we were married in the church where we had met under the Cross of Christ. Dorothy baked the bread and I purchased the Mateus wine for communion.

We honeymooned in Galveston for a week. One afternoon my father came down and took us fishing. Dorothy caught a six and a half pound speckled trout off the south jetties. From the balcony of the beach house, we threw pennies for good luck in the canal. We have had plenty of that. As to life's unexpected bad luck, heartbreaks and deaths along the way, our love and God's Angels have always supported and carried us to a deeper, more sacred place.

Following the honeymoon in Galveston, we packed up and moved to Austin to attend law school. Classes started on June 6, 1972. I have since joked with others we were married on May 20, 1972, and went to law school for the honeymoon.

In writing this chapter, I have reflected on the more than forty years since that blessing in the sacrament of marriage. Dorothy and I have been true to and for each other. Our biblical journeys together and apart have been sources of strength and validation. We have seen that God and all of His Angels who brought us together have never left our midst. Dorothy kept me steady in law school, pushed me to class, sat with me in all of my examinations to transcribe my dictation. She has mothered our two children, John and Catherine and our grandchildren, Tristan, Ellora, Ellisa and John V (affectionately called Jax).

Her love for me has been miraculous. Every time that I have been sick, fearful, worried, troubled, or hurt, Dorothy has had the healing gift to say the right words or do just the perfect thing to immediately put me in a better place. That has to be the power of God's Love shining through her—my Angel acting in God's grace.

Just as it was no accident that God selected such a special mother as Lucile for a son with polio, Mother's footprints in my heart were and are filled by the love and loving acts of my dearest Dorothy.

This morning I awoke from deep sleep. My eyes opened. I looked up and saw Charles Schorre's *Bending Angel* on the wall above our bed. I glanced down and saw my Angel Dorothy sleeping beside me. With my right index finger I gently pressed on her forehead the Cross of Christ. I said to my sleeping beauty, "Dorothy, may God bless you in the name of the Father, the Son and the Holy Ghost. In the beginning you were my best friend. Then, you were my one true love. God brought our two souls together. At the altar our two hearts became one with God's everlasting Love. You were and are my tender, sweet lover. Now, you are my forever Angel. May God bless you, my wife, my Angel, my true love forever. Amen."

CHAPTER 11

The Iron Lung Angel

Part of God's plan was for me to become a lawyer to help families in the throes of divorce. Through this work I have endeavored to bring to them some of the bright hope and unflagging belief that I have found through my faith in God and His Divine will. It was, and is, my passion to help families heal. To use who I am and whose I am to help couples divide the fruit of their labors. To share their children as blessed treasures from God.

Yet through the fall of 1984 and 1985's early spring, I had been so consumed with caring for my clients that I had not been caring for me. Thirty years after the onset of polio, I became aware that a change was taking place within me. Something was out of place, out of balance, much like people must feel in a marriage about to crack open.

The pieces did not fit. The mosaic of my world was out of harmony. I could no longer work at the same harried pace. I felt new limitations on the days and nights of my life. I didn't know that the voice that had told me in rehabilitation to work harder, to ignore pain, that voice that had pulled me out of the nethermost hellish pit of paralysis in my younger years, was now spinning a lie for me to follow downward to the grave.

I was determined to become that warrior-child again, to win through sheer determination and will—just like spouses who believe a marriage can be saved no matter what, like spouses who think with the right judge, the correct political pull, or the well-chosen tenacious litigator, the result will be reconciliation and love restored. The mystery of marriage is that it is so much more than a legal relationship. Without heart, it is nothing.

I was not going to listen to my need for rest nor ask a doctor for help. Rather, I declared war. I worked even harder at my office—nights, days, and weekends. I committed to daily strenuous exercise rather than resting when my body felt the need. I purchased a Schwinn Exercycle and peddled four miles every day. I walked by foot on shell roads in Emmottville, one-half mile each day under fifty-year-old live oaks which hovered over me like mythical black vultures waiting for their prey to collapse in total exhaustion. At work, I consumed frequent glasses of iced tea to get over the polio wall with the temporary escape ladder provided by caffeine. In burning the candle at both ends, I had twice the light; but, the candle of my life was being expended twice as rapidly to the point of physical exhaustion and death's doorstep.

The soul does not believe in nor need control. Control is an illusion. For, in the end, we discover the truth that each of us must live out the mystery of our misery and calling. We suffer illness and learn its consequences, like paralysis, deformity, pain, and scars. We choose to love our husbands and wives, and then learn love's consequences, like joy, children, heartbreak, or even divorce. Health, like love in marriage, can end as mysteriously as it begins.

I fell from my illusion of control in March 1985. I had come to the inevitable end of my long walks and Exercycle rides down the road to nowhere.

As I drove home on Fairbanks-North Houston Road, one mile from my home, panic struck me. I felt a cold, wet, invisible fluid running down my left arm, but my shirt sleeve was dry. My chest felt tight. There was a tingling over my breastplate. Short and rapid breaths.

I called home. Dorothy answered. I said I was in trouble. I hoped to be home in a few minutes and we'd leave for the hospital immediately when I got there.

I was admitted to the cardiac care unit. I underwent an EKG. Despite my invisible respiratory fatigue at my admission, the attending physician ordered a respiratory function test. This test was conducted in a capsule that resembled an egg with a chair in it. Because my vital lung capacity as a result of polio at best was 1250cc, the technicians could not get a good reading. The test was repeated over and over again which further depleted my reserves of strength.

That testing was followed by a test for blood gases. Getting blood from me for purposes of study is like finding a needle in a hay stack. Over and over again the technician kept sticking the needle on the back of my hands to locate venous blood. After thirty minutes of probing with the needle, enough blood was obtained to determine the oxygen and carbon dioxide saturation levels in my blood.

Then my attending physician ordered a bone scan to be done by injecting radioactive fluid into my veins. I had read recently that a patient in Florida had been given what was thought to be radioactive material for a bone scan. Unfortunately, the substance injected caused the patient's death. The technician was not happy with me asking him what he was injecting me with and if he had verified the contents.

I was returned to my bed. At that point, I was a limp wash rag of pain and fatigue. The doctor came in a few minutes later and said, "Jack, you have had a heart attack. Please do not worry because the heart attack occurred quite some time ago and your heart has healed. However, from the bone scan it appears to me you are missing several ribs in your back." I asked, "Why are my ribs missing?" The doctor replied," You have a degenerative bone disease. I do not know what it is. More tests will be needed to be done."

After the doctor left, a technician came into the room. He said," I want to put a Hep-Lock on your left neck and shoulder. The Hep-Lock will be used to inject life-saving medicine if you have further heart trouble." At that point, I refused. Dorothy did not push the issue with me.

When the room was emptied of medical personnel, I looked at Dorothy and said, "We need to get out against doctor's orders. If I stay in the hospital, they are going to kill me." My dear, sweet Dorothy took me home.

At home, I called my polio doctor. Within a day or two I was admitted to TIRR (The Institute of Rehabilitation and Research). Dr. Vallbona looked over my medical records. The wisdom of my decision to go to TIRR was immediately demonstrated.

Dr. Vallbona said, "Jack, you have not had a heart attack. The cardiologist who read the EKG at that hospital did not take your severe scoliosis into account. The EKG I had done shows that your heart is perfectly normal."

"What about my degenerative bone disease and missing ribs?" I asked. Dr. Vallbona then chuckled and said, "The radiologist did not know that three of your ribs had been removed and used by Dr. Harrington to fuse your spine when he installed the three steel rods."

Gone was the wall of worry over two misdiagnoses. My hope was given wings.

I learned I suffered from post-polio syndrome, including respiratory fatigue and physical exhaustion. This syndrome (PPS) was affecting one-third of the over 300,000 polio survivors who lived in America. Untreated, I would die of right-sided heart failure.

My fears spun out of control. Fear of a tracheotomy, of extended hospitalization, reduced work hours and lost income, separation from loved ones, dependence on others, and then death.

Now, my walking shoes and Exercycle were put away, just as my bicycle with training wheels had been put in the garage when I left for Hedgecroft Hospital in Houston at the age of six. I tried to adjust to the realities of what I must face—the newest set of hard life-lessons. I tried to believe that learning those lessons was necessary to allow my soul to release the coil of potentiality still remaining in the mystery of my being and my suffering. But it was difficult, just as it is difficult for divorcing couples, living and growing through times of catastrophe and the death of their relationship, who try to believe that learning new unwanted lessons will someday result in happiness and wholeness.

Now, for me to do less was to do more for my health. To bend and go where God's Angels and my disease led me was far healthier than to adhere to the rigidity of my relentless work ethic. Learning to fly like an Angel and experiencing free-falling from the heights of my fears were better for my spirit and health than my constantly clawing uphill to find solid ground.

After a series of unsuccessful attempts to ease my respiratory fatigue, I was left with three choices: (1) a tracheotomy with scarring, disfigurement, and ventilator dependence; (2) the Iron Lung; or (3) death.

In prayer, an Angel's voice spoke to me. "As a child of God you are an instrument, a vessel, which carries God's Love from Heaven to the Earth. Enter the Iron Lung. Use it as my instrument, as my vessel to hold and heal you in God's Grace. Step into the darkness. In it, you will be able to see the light of God's love for you. You will find a deeper faith in God and in yourself."

Because of this Angel's message, I chose the Iron Lung; or rather, the Iron Lung chose me.

Prior to that time, the closest I ever came to being in the Lung was in the spring of 1955 when I had pneumonia and respiratory exhaustion.

My mom always stood watch over me when I was ill. She must have learned two lessons about being my parent. The first lesson was being awake when her child needed a parent. The second lesson was learning the warning signs of respiratory fatigue. When I was sick and asleep in bed and breathing with great difficulty, I would wake up, roll over and look at the bedroom door behind me. My mother would be standing there like an Angel watching over me. She stood quietly with a Rolex watch in her hand. (My father had given her that watch when he returned from World War II.) Mom would look at my chest to count my breaths. When the number of breaths per minute reached a certain number, it was time for a trip to the hospital. Mom would say to my father, "Jack, get dressed and start the car. Bubba must go to the hospital now!"

On this particular night, I was rushed to Hedgecroft Hospital by two fearful parents, then was rolled on my stretcher into a room on the second floor. I saw a yellow metallic monster ready to consume me. I gave no thought to the help the Lung would give me. I knew that if I was locked in there I would never get out. Worse, I would die in there, my living body placed in a metal casket prior to my internment. I screamed, "Don't put me in the Iron Lung! Mommy and Daddy, don't let them do it to me!" Tears. Screaming. As the two male attendants lifted me off the stretcher, I reached out with all the strength left in my tiny arms and grasped the post of a brown upright floor lamp close by in final defiance of this metal creature. My parents were so upset by my reaction that they stood between the Lung and me and aborted my confinement in the Tank.

For that night, I was spared from entombment in that Iron Lung. Instead, I was hooked up to a Monighan Respirator. The attendants laid me in bed. Then, they placed a cuirass or plastic shell over my chest. The shell was held tightly against my tired chest and abdominal wall by two straps wrapped around my back. A long hose leading from a motor was secured to the shell. The respirator was turned on and caused an intermittent vacuum to occur inside the shell—a vacuum which lifted my rib cage. To save a life, through the gift of breath, is the respirator's purpose.

In 1955, thousands of polio victims, like me, lay beached in their hospital beds like turtles with their stiff Monighan respirator shells to protect them and guard their vulnerable insides. Later I would come to know the beauty and life force evidenced by Ridley turtles. Much, much later I would come to understand the spiritual necessity of the human patience required to receive God's gifts, including His loving kindness. That same loving kindness He gives to us all in our life experiences including tragedy.

In seeking to live the spiritual life, the imagery of my shell-like appearance of a Ridley Turtle proved to be insightful in another way as well. In 1954, at the age of six, I did not know the importance of sticking one's neck out. I learned that later from my parents, Jack and Lucile, when they acted contrary to the admonitions of my primary physician when he told them that I would not survive the surgery to insert Harrington steel rods in my back to prevent further scoliosis or curvature of the spine.

Instead, they acted on the advice of an innovative orthopedic surgeon, Doctor Paul R. Harrington, who told them that I would survive the four and a half hour surgery, and those rods would extend my life. My parents stuck their necks out for me. They took a risk, a chance for me to live a much longer, more useful life. The hope contained within that risk of my death outweighed the paralysis of indecision. Sticking their necks out was far better than my inevitable death at age fourteen from complications of scoliosis and deformity.

God asks us every day, "Are you prepared to stick your neck out to do God's work for others? Or will you stay in your comfortable shell?"

Emotional shells can protect us and our soft insides from harm, or they can isolate us from doing the right thing. Oftentimes in life and love, good deeds and healthy outcomes seem just as rare as those Ridley Turtles have become. A Ridley Turtle instinctively knows it must risk sticking its neck out. To eat? To see where it is going on its journey? As children of God we are asked to develop a natural instinct to care for our own souls by caring for the souls of others.

Before polio, I remember visiting an eight-year old girl, Margaret Ariola, with my mother. The girl lived in a small white-frame farmhouse her father had built for his family. Not the hardened hands of Mr. Batiste Ariola, her father, nor the constant vigil of her loving mother could save her from polio— the paralysis, the Iron Lung, or her death a few years later. At the age of four in 1952, I recall walking up the steps of the Ariola farmhouse with my mother, Lucile, and a plate of fresh homemade chocolate chip cookies. As I walked inside the house, my innocent eyes enlarged in horror at seeing a pretty girl in the small living room lying inside an Iron Lung. In the reflection of the mirror above my head and below her I saw she made an effort to smile at me, to pretend for my sake that everything was normal in her strange existence. I knew otherwise, just like children who can see through the veil of their parents' conflict before a divorce is filed. I held my mother's hand tighter. I was grateful for a mother like her and for a life that would never confine my body in such a machine.

With the onset of polio at age six, the innocence of that young boy died; with the onset of the late effects of polio at age thirty-six, I lost the life to which I had become accustomed.

My mind and spirit struggled to stay out of the Lung with the same tenaciousness as the child with pneumonia who clung to the floor lamp in that hospital room in 1955. Yet, the Iron Lung was as imperative for me as a divorce is for mothers and fathers, husbands and wives, sons and daughters, who absolutely need a legal end to relationships irretrievably broken, who need separate households for healthy healing, who need to share their children instead of divide them like property, who could not save their marriages with prayer and God's help.

Could I have lived without the Iron Lung? Can broken couples survive their journey into the dark and uncertain territory of divorce? What treasures can they find in the darkness? What treasures would I find in the darkness?

I imagine I viewed the Iron Lung like couples view divorce. A voyage to purgatory. A journey downward. They fear they will not survive the process, that the dark tunnel is devoid of life, support, and, most importantly, the love that spun the marriage into being. Just as I was unable to see the light at the end of my metal tunnel, oftentimes couples cannot see the light which resolution can provide at the end of their divorces. For me in the Tank, and for them in divorce, not going in means never having to worry about getting out. Fear fuels resistance.

How do people feel about being dragged into divorce when they have struggled and fought to save a fallen marriage and/or denied its overwhelming problems? They probably felt the same as I did—a survivor of decades of hard work and painful recovery forced by post-polio syndrome into the Iron Lung. It was not fair, not what I wanted, not what I deserved. I felt twice cursed. Thirty-five years after polio, my worst fears became a living nightmare.

In response to an Angel's invitation, I prayed to God to answer questions I thought I would never have to ask. How could I enter the Iron Lung in a sacred way—how could I enter the Metal Beast, a kind of "metaphysical" belly of growth and experience like Jonah's whale, and grow in my relationship to God?

How would I spend countless lost precious hours separated from a warm marriage bed or evenings with family in this time of confinement? Could I, like Terry Waite imprisoned in Lebanon or Nelson Mandela in South Africa, use this nightly confinement in the Lung to learn about the truly important things in life, about the sacred, in such extraordinary solitude? How could I work all day outside the Lung to use up all the energy I had in reserve in service to others in the practice of matrimonial law, and return home to my unwanted metal house? How could I spend ten to twelve hours in the Tank, physically separated from family, who were enjoying life in other rooms of our house? How could I miss reading bedtime stories late at night to my nine-year old son, John, or my six-year old daughter, Catherine?

What would my Tank time do to my wife, Dorothy, or our children? Would they suffer like divorcing parents who long for affection, their hearts deadened by separation from loved ones, their lives marked by the stigmata of the painful wounds of divorce?

Could my Iron Lung become a cathedral, a mosque, a synagogue, a cocoon, a metallic womb, a place to surround and nurture my wounds, my respiratory fatigue? A place to retreat, to grow inside of, to learn from, to pray and worship in, to find my undiscovered self, to find God? Could it become a place from which to be reborn from each day?

So, on an ordinary evening one night in March of 1986, I spent my first of 1,884 nights alone in the Iron Lung. That first of many nights in the hospital and later at home in the Iron Lung began a journey into darkness, separation, fear, aloneness, and grief. This was the kind of geography that God uses as food for our souls to grow. God knows that a catastrophe, death, or loss is a terrible thing to waste.

As I wrestled with my time in the Tank, I kept hearing the voice of an Angel, "Know that you are loved. Know that you are not alone in the darkness. God has a plan for you in the darkness, in the Iron Lung, and in your life. God has sent you an Angel and an Iron Lung. Both are instruments of my Love and healing. Prayerfully submit to the darkness. You will learn lessons in the dark that you will never learn in the light." After many nights of prayer, I began to appreciate the beauty and meaning of this metallic soul-scape, so much like a sparse desert, a deep cavern, the stark flatlands of Dakota, or the nave of a tiny church.

The attendants laid me on the table bed and rolled it inside the Lung. My head stuck out through the opening at the end. The sound of the large curved iron bars locking me inside signaled the beginning of my confinement. I thought the sound was like prison bars closing behind me. I pushed back the tears, like divorcing couples who are grieving for their dead marriages and broken dreams. The attendant secured my neck with the twist collar, spinning it clockwise ever tighter, as the twist collar of divorce often chokes wives and husbands.

At night, I often wondered if there was another purpose for the tight seal around my neck, something more than to preserve the integrity of the vacuum inside the chamber. I wondered whether the yellow twist collar was a yoke or a cleric's collar for my soul to let me know the purpose of the weight I was to carry as father, husband, lawyer, and community servant. Was it a yoke—to let me know, to help me discern, to help me recall and remember who I was and whose I am? Could I carry this burden long enough to see a deeper reason or purpose of my being? Of my suffering?

The motor turned on and created a vacuum inside the chamber. Was this vacuum, which forced me to take sixteen breaths each minute whether I wanted them or not, like the vacuum in divorce—a vacuum which not only sucks out my clients' limited finances and their hope to resolve their own plight with God's help? Could this vacuum create in its happening and its aftermath an empty place where room is made for me to fill with faith, hope, growth, resolution, and even epiphany? Strangely, in that vacuum, I began to hear the Angel's voice more clearly.

For a while, the electric motor of the Lung seemed to get louder each night. Even during my office days away from the Lung I thought, at times, I could hear it waiting for me to come home. The murmur of a whale, the tick of the clock in the belly of the crocodile that waited for Captain Hook or just the sounds of a church's bell tower—sounds of an Angel's invitation: "The doors are open. Come into the House of God."

The air rushed past my ears, down my neck, and on past my chilled shoulders each time a breath was taken. After a few nights in the hospital, the yellow monster invaded my bedroom at home. I laid there many nights wondering why this was happening to me. Sometimes late at night, I wondered whether that rush of wind past my ears contained the voice of an Angel whispering God's answers to my prayers.

Some nights in the winter in the Lung, it got very cold in the darkened Tank. I discovered that a light bulb could be turned on to warm the inner chamber. A light in the darkness. My kids placed stickers, magnets, and drawings on the head plate of my Tank—to transform my metal house into a decorated home. All were beacons in the chilly blackness.

My 1,884 nights in the Iron Lung were more than the geography I have described. My tank on wheels functioned, just as a person's journey through divorce may function, as a vehicle on an unwanted inward journey. It showed what else I could learn from adversity. It revealed what I could learn not only in spite of, but also because of, wounds, brokenness, and suffering.

The Iron Lung began as my enemy. But the Tank soon became my timeless and eternal teacher, taking me deeper into the realm of the soul. Closer to God, His Angels and Archangels.

The Iron Lung left my bedroom in April of 1992. In an eternal and everlasting way, it will always be there—unseen but present in my home, in the courtroom, in my office, in the words I write and in my heart. As the men wheeled the Lung onto the bed of the truck, it left fully adorned with five years of stickers left by my kids. Stickers which brightened the dark horizon of my night skies—acts of love which make houses into homes. Such acts of love make our own crucifixions, divorces, illnesses, tragedies, and catastrophes, all survivable, endurable for God's own unique mysterious purposes.

Now, in my calling as a family lawyer, when I see horror and grief in a face or the wooden look of an abused woman, or see the fear that love and inherent goodness are being consumed in the process of a bitter divorce, that unseen six-year old polio victim is right there with them struggling for dignity and control, desperately hanging onto hope as I hung on to that floor lamp. That unseen thirty-six-year-old attorney in the Tank is there too. Because the Iron Lung was my teacher in adulthood, I believe I am at my very best in my calling because I have really been at my very worst.

Prior to the time my Tank departed Emmottville, this teacher had also become my friend. Instead of considering this machine as something foreign, hostile, threatening, or unwanted, I heard an Angel's voice, a message from God, that changed this experience. As a miracle of sorts, I was transformed in the process too. Just as humankind is a reflection of the sacred, the eternal and the Divine, I imagined the Lung with its metal skin as part of my body. It was flesh of my flesh, skin of my skin. Its breath was my breath. Its life made my life possible. It became a safe, nurturing place to accept my body and soul at the end of the day, a cocoon-like, comforting, healing place for me to be renewed for the dawn of the next day. It became an inseparable part of me. I could not live and do my calling without it, and it had no purpose to serve without me, my body and my adversity.

To God, everyone is part of everything. Every child is part of God's Kingdom, flesh of God's flesh, breath of God's breath. In the darkness of my long nights in the Iron Lung, God's Love warmed me. God lit up my life with Heavenly Grace. In prayer, my journey in the Iron Lung carried me to a more sacred place. The Lung seemed to move me to this deeper place on the wings of an Angel.

Instead of moving on its wheels, I imagined the wheels of the Lung were the feet of Christ carrying the cross to Calvary or the feet of a saint, a martyr, a soldier in battle, or the paws of a lion taking me to a place I needed to be as a Child of God. It was a place I am so thankful I found.

Sometimes we must be alone in the darkness to hear the voice of an Angel who bends over us and to see the Light of Christ.

CHAPTER 12

Brother Angel Charles, the Disciple of Mother's Plans

I still remember lying in my parents' upstairs bedroom under a ceiling fan's breeze when Dr. Sterling told my parents that his testing had just shown I had polio. Even though I had a high fever, I recall so many details—the chenille bedspread, the sweltering August heat, and my parents' embrace as they leaned into each other and against a bedroom wall when the devastating news was delivered.

None of us, least of all me, understood all that would be asked of us as a family in the coming years as we went forward on the path God had chosen for us. But several things are stunningly clear to me in hindsight.

One of those truths is that my younger brother Charlie, who was not quite five years old when I was struck with polio, was and is my Angel Brother.

You see, Charles and I were best friends before polio and stayed best friends afterwards. Even though so many of both of our dreams died because of the polio, we were able to experience the blessed riches of our relationship and find other dreams to fulfill.

Let me tell you about my Angel Brother Charles.

As part of my mother's and God's plan, Charles gave up the opportunity to be a child for another year so that he could enter school with me. As I was moved into Hedgecroft Hospital, Charles was taken to Aunt Midge and Uncle Otis's house on Bingle Road near Long Point Road. As the Hillendahl men were plowing their nearby farm fields to grow corn, fruit and vegetables, Charles was cultivating a year of hard school work in first grade at Ridgecrest Elementary even though he should have been in kindergarten. Mother's sister, Midge, tended to Charlie's needs but she was not his mother, nor was Uncle Otis his father. Aunt Midge and Uncle Otis' son, Philip, was Charlie's roommate. Yet, Philip was not a brother. In those times when a five-year old boy needed a mother and father during the week for consolation, treating an injury, or assisting with homework, Charles knew that his mom and dad were tending to me instead.

At the end of the year at Ridgecrest, Charles gave up something else—the right to be in classes independently and not have to care for me. Not only in the classroom at school and extracurricular activities, but also at home. Charles had much bigger responsibilities in taking care of me than being just who he was, a child of six.

As the years progressed, our family struggled to live our unconventional life in the most conventional way possible. Charles, by his deeds, said to me "I am strong for you, Bubba. My arms, my hands, and my fingers are yours. I will do with them what you cannot do for yourself. I will dress you. I will bathe you. I will give you your medicine. I will cast your fishing rod. I will bait your hook. I will catch the baseball for you. I will bat the ball for you. I will run the bases for you. I will knock the croquette ball as far as I can for you. I will sit you down on the pew at church. I will stand you up. I will walk you to the communion rail and help you kneel. I will lift you up on your feet after you have taken the bread and wine. Like our mom and dad I will pick you up when you fall. Then, I will dust you off and help you try to learn to walk again. I will not ever leave you alone."

Through the years, Charles' deeds also expressed that "my legs are yours too. I will give therapy to your legs so that they might move like mine. I will do your household chores as well as mine so that you never feel that you are not contributing to the family when you are home. I will hold your arm as you walk across the graduation stage at Cy-Fair High School as we accept our high school diplomas from the superintendent of the school district. I will drive the car on your dates with girls when you do not have the ability to drive. As you are my best friend, I will also be your Best Man. As Best Man I will stand proudly next to you on your wedding day and celebrate not only true love but what you have done to overcome that which I escaped."

And yet, with all that my Angel Brother has done for me, I have heard him say that he has regrets that he didn't do more. This surprises me. Perhaps, it shouldn't because I have regrets as well, when it comes to my brother. Some of my regrets have to do with polio; some do not.

Once, at the age of eight, I took it upon myself to take Charlie's silver cowboy cap pistol in my hand. I took a screwdriver out of a drawer in my dad's barn. My job for the day was to take the pistol apart piece by piece, to dissect it, digest it, to figure how it worked and put it all back together again in the same condition as I had found it. This process would surely be a piece of cake. I set the pistol on the kitchen table next to the screwdriver. Without my mother being present to see what I was doing, I took out the screws and laid them carefully on the table. I took out the trigger and its spring. Then, the revolving bullet chamber. I was so careful. I had to remember how to put the pistol back together again just as I had found it. Charles would never know I had taken his pistol.

To my frustration and horror, I learned it was much easier to take something apart than to put it back together again, just like my recovery from polio. Polio had left my healthy parts disconnected. Then, came the hard work and the lessons. The reconstruction of the pistol mirrored my rehabilitation after polio. Good intentions and techniques are still worthwhile, but they may not accomplish what was intended. The way the pieces were envisioned to fit back together often does not turn out to be functional, pretty, or in the original condition.

After an hour of frustration, I went to my mother and confessed. I asked if she could save me from my foolishness. Following the example of every good mother in history, she chastised me for taking someone else's property without permission. Of course, she was right. I needed to apologize to Charlie when he came home from school and ask him for forgiveness. That was his pistol, not mine. I had thought, "What would he mind anyway?" I would put it back like I found it. He would never know anyway. My mother, my father, and even Charles were not able to put the pistol back together either.

When I confessed to Charles, you could see the disappointment and anger on his face. But like so many other times, there were no complaints from his lips. It seemed as though this was just another burden that went along with having a brother with polio. Even then I knew that polio was no excuse for letting my brother down.

But there is one story I'd like to tell you about Charles' and my closeness. You would think that with forty-five first cousins confined to the same piece of property as large as one hundred acres, there would be too much room for bruised egos. Peace would always prevail. And, in fact, for the most part, we got along well. But occasionally, as we grew older, the cousins exchanged fighting words and a fight ensued. Usually over some game of sport, kick the can or baseball in the front of Aunt Mabel's house.

Before a cousins' baseball game after school one day, Charles tilted my non-motorized Everest & Jennings wheelchair on its big back wheels and pushed me down the dirt road and parked it in front of the northeast corner of Aunt Mabel's and Uncle Howard's home and five-acre lot. We cousins enjoyed playing baseball there.

The outfield fence (over which a homerun needed to be hit) was a line of pine trees fifty feet tall a block away. When a ball sailed over those pine trees, we treated the batter as if Babe Ruth had done it again. This was a great venue for baseball as Aunt Mabel was a fabulous cook. She had dishes of candy positioned strategically all over the house. A cousin need not step into the front door more than a foot or two to grab a handful of candy and quickly return to the baseball game. If a player needed his thirst quenched, parched in the rigors of a sun-filled afternoon, there was always a classic pitcher of Kool Aid with enormous quantities of sugar in it. Aunt Mabel was raising six kids. She did not have time to supervise our outdoor play unless there was a true, devastating emergency. Aunt Mabel could never imagine how such a crisis would ever occur in the first place. If a boy got hurt, it was a lesson to be learned. Boys did not cry and each boy needed to man up.

On this day, the cousins were left to their own devices.

My brother Charles, my cousins Bob and Howard all got along well. We had another cousin (let's call him Freddie) who had a chip on his shoulder. When things did not go Freddie's way, he was difficult to deal with. We were playing baseball. At a critical moment in the game, Charles tagged out Freddie at home plate and called him out. Freddie thought the call was wrong and that he had scored at home plate.

Charles knew otherwise. Right must prevail. The wrong result, just to appease Freddie, could not be tolerated. There are reasons why great societies disintegrate. A decline in morals and values overtake the fabric of society. Charles was convinced that allowing this wrong to replace the right call would set in motion an infectious disease to ruin his beloved Emmottville. Freddie let Charlie know that he was prepared to fight him if Charles refused to change the call. I so wish he had.

As if there was a Floyd Patterson boxing match taking place at Madison Square Garden, the cousins cheered Charles and Freddie on and on. I was too upset to recognize which side the cousins were cheering for. Aunt Mabel looked out the screen door. I called her to my brother's aid as he was on the short side of the fight at the time. She poked her head out the door and just went back inside the house.

Charles was strong but not as scrappy as Freddie. Freddie fought dirty to win. He knew how to kick for the gonads and punch in the face. Charlie suffered a blow to the face, another blow to his gut, and then he went to the ground. He struggled to get up. Freddie sat on top of him.

I screamed for one of my cousins to stop cheering and help Charlie. To my dismay, they continued to cheer even more. Now they were cheering for Charles, but he was in a very bad spot. There had been rain the day before. The ditch behind home plate was filled with a few inches of water and slimy mud. As Charlie struggled to extricate himself from Freddie's weight on top of him, Freddie flipped him over and put his two hands behind Charlie's ears. He shoved Charles' face into the muddy water. I could not do anything. Freddie better be glad I had polio. If I was able-bodied, there is no telling what I would have done to him that day.

I started yelling and screaming at Freddie to get off my brother. "Freddie! Freddie, you're killing him! He's going to drown! Think what you're doing." Suddenly the heat of the moment broke into silence. Freddie said to Charles, "Charles, if I let you up, are we done?" Charles looked at him and nodded his head yes in agreement. Freddie looked at Charles covered in mud from head to toe with pieces of grass poking out of his nose and mud around his mouth and lips. Freddie said, "Have you had enough?"

Then something happened which was exquisitely, unexpectedly beautiful and just. Charles had cocked his right arm back. As Freddie's words "have you had enough?" had just finished resonating, with one beautiful blow, Charles' right fist struck Freddie's nose. It appeared it might be broken. Blood spilled down Freddie's face.

Freddie screamed, "Charles, look what you've done! How could you have done this to me! I'm going to go tell my mommy!" To which Charles responded, "Go ahead, you little crybaby." Our cowardly, insensitive cousins who had not intervened earlier started cheering, laughing, and watching Freddie with his bloody nose and tail tucked between his legs running home to Mama. Everyone left on the field looked at each other. The bigger, more important game was over. The winner was Charles. His strong right hand had righted the wrong.

Charles tilted my wheelchair back to roll me home. I

wept as Charles wheeled my chair, a wheelbarrow full of tears, home. I so wished that I could have done more to help him.

Maybe boys do such things in their rites of passage to find their own way to adulthood. Boys will be boys. But Charles was not just any boy. Charles was my best friend. Best friends never deserve enduring such an event to serve as a rite of passage. As Charles rolled the wheelchair into our home, I apologized to him: "I am so sorry I could not have done more. If I had not had polio, I would have beaten the shit out of Freddie for you." Charles said, "Bubba, don't mind. I'm okay. Freddie's going home to his Mama like a big baby. I'm taking my big brother home who is more grown up than Freddie will ever be."

Occasional fights between cousins were never as great as the brotherhood we shared. Freddie's nose and hurt feelings healed. As mad as I was at Freddie that dark day, Freddie, Charles and I managed to navigate adolescence and had fun times fishing, double dating and playing many rounds of miniature golf. I am also indebted to Freddie for saving my life. At the age of 19 during a game of Put-Put golf, I stepped off a concrete pad and slipped on a slimy patch of Coca Cola. As the base of my skull swiftly fell towards the sharp edge of the concrete pad, behind me Freddie lunged forward. With less than a foot to spare his two strong hands caught the back of my head. Otherwise, I would have had a serious life-threatening brain injury.

Brother Charles knew long before mainstreaming of the disabled into the general population that his brother, Bubba, should have the opportunity to participate in or-dinary manly activities. Male-bonding. Food-gathering. Hunting. Burping. Farting. Drinking too much. Ignoring all familial obligations to escape to the world of testosterone-induced fishing trips. Tomorrow can wait. Today is the essence of the moment. Now is forever.

Because of polio, Charles was concerned that I had not experienced the joys of fishing in the surf. Sand and wind blowing in one's face from off an island on the coast south of New Orleans and the Mississippi delta. Salty smells in the nostrils of the nose. Skin parched in the sun. Sand in one's shorts followed by the worrisome itching, stinging, and burning. Such were the rigors and the worthwhile, endurable consequences of being a true man. The land where male chests are full of hair. Muscles are bulging. Men do what men have done since the dawn of Man's creation--- fishing, hunting and food-gathering.

Dad had taken my brother Charles to the Chandeliers barrier islands. Their catch was limitless. The ice boxes returned full of fish. When the ice boxes did not have any more room, then the fish were thrown into large garbage cans and packed with ice. I had asked Charles to tell me what it was like to wade-fish on Little Gosher Island.

Charles wanted me to give me more than words. He wanted me to have as near a true-to-life experience as was possible for me. Careful plans were made by Charles. I was invited. I would go. How could I turn down Charlie's offer to accompany him and my cousin, Howard, on this trip of a lifetime? Dad said Charles could take his Proline boat, motor and trailer. Dad let Charles know that the trailer had three balding tires. I heard Charles and Howard debate whether it was safe to travel such a distance with tires in such condition. But, with God with us, surely the tires would last on the journey to New Orleans and back. There was no need to be concerned. There were two spares.

The tackle was made ready. No corks for us. No live or dead bait. True fishermen, especially the Emmott men, never used bait. We used only artificial lures. If the fish took the bait, it was not because it was fresh. It was not because the bait moved because it was alive. It was not because it stunk so much it attracted catfish and other undesirable fish lower in the food chain. Rather, the fish were caught solely because of the skill of the fisherman reeling in the line at the right speed and with the perfect stroke. The right twist, the right pull and the right jerk at the right time. The right feel at the right moment when the hook was set by arms yanking the tip of the fishing rod heavenward and setting the hook into the lips of a fish that would never have a chance to get away.

As Charlie loaded up all of the supplies, tackle boxes and rods and reels in the back of the Proline boat, I noticed there was a brown pontoon-like vessel about six feet long. A boat seat was mounted in the middle between the pontoons. A seatbelt was affixed to the seat. A seventy-five foot rope was attached to the nose of the vessel. I carefully read the logo on the vessel – "Bass Buster". I asked Charles what plans he had for the Bass Buster. With great pride Charles said, "Bubba, the Bass Buster will provide you with an experience that will give you a taste of what it is like to walk in the surf. To wade amidst the crabs, fingerling fish, and occasional shark. I know your legs are too weak to walk in the surf. So, I will strap you in the chair. You will be safe and secure. I will put a life jacket on you. Then I will tie that long, long rope to my waist. I will pull you through the surf as if we are wade fishing in step with one another. This is the closest to the real thing that I have come up with to give you a true to life experience. It ought to be wonderful." I was convinced. That sounded so well planned, how could I refuse my brother, Charles?

It was midafternoon on a Friday. The three of us had left

work early. The gear was ready. By the time we had reached Beaumont, a tire had exploded on the trailer. Howard exclaimed, "I knew we should have replaced the tires before we left Houston!" Charles said, "Howard, never mind. I've got a spare. We are prepared. Let's change the tire quickly so we can still make it to New Orleans on time." Howard and Charles took off the tire that had exploded and put on another tire, one of the two spares. As we approached Baton Rouge, a second tire on the trailer blew. Before Howard could say anything, Charles said, "Howard, don't worry. I've got a second spare. Surely, we won't need a third. We have better luck than that." Howard responded, "Let's move quickly. We still have a chance to get to New Orleans before 10:30 PM. That's when things really get going on Bourbon Street." I sat in the back seat looking at the two of them, my dear sweet brother, Charlie, and my cousin, Howard. I looked at them like I was watching a preview of a movie from the back seat of a car at a drive-in movie theater. Was the scene going to be the trip to Hell and back, or surf fishing at its best? Just as we approached Metairie on Interstate 10, a third tire on the trailer flattened. We heard the "Thump, Thump, Thump". Charles stated the obvious, "We're in trouble. Let's find a filling station which is open and buy a tire from them. Then we can spend at least an hour or so on Bourbon Street." Rolling along at ten miles an hour, we limped our way into New Orleans. It was after 10:30pm. All the filling stations with tire services were closed. There was a 24-hour filling station, an Exxon, in the heart of New Orleans, but its tire shop did not open until seven in the morning. We were stranded. Instead of enjoying the delights of Bourbon Street, we tried to sleep and waited for the tire shop to open. Charlie, being the eternal optimist, said, "Don't worry. Men, we didn't really come here to go to Bourbon Street. We came here to fish." The tire was purchased. Fortunately, Howard had enough money in his wallet to cover the cost.

We drove a while down the Mississippi delta to a town, Old Shell Beach in Saint Bernard Parish. Charles and Howard slipped the boat off the trailer into the Mississippi River Gulf Outlet Canal. Charles gave the Mercury outboard motor full throttle and steered the boat southeast toward the Gulf of Mexico. The conditions were perfect. The screech of seagulls. The large brown pelicans flying overhead like military aircraft carrying cargo. The sound of other boat traffic. The push of the water against the bow of the boat, which split the surface of the water into a rolling "V" wave behind the boat. The purr of the Mercury motor on all cylinders driving the boat toward the Chandelier Islands, and the surf fishing Charlie had promised me. The winds were calm. The skies, baby blue. Not a cloud above. The water was in perfect condition and clear. We made our way to the Chandelier and Big and Little Gosher Islands in about 45 minutes. As Charles steered the boat around the south side of Little Gosher, the bait fish boiled on the water's surface. The bait fish pelted the surface causing it to look like bubble wrap. Occasionally, the trout, red fish and mackerel hit the boiling surface, striking the bait fish and sending their schoolmates under the water. This canvas seemed ideal for the picture Charles had painted in his special plans for me.

We buttered ourselves up with sunscreen. Put on our sunglasses. Our long-sleeved shirts. We wore baseball caps on our heads. The anchor was pitched by Howard over the nose of the boat. With our boat secured, Howard and Charles pushed the Bass Buster into the water. Charles and Howard lifted me out of the boat and set me onto the seat of the Bass Buster. Charles said with authority, "Stay still, Bubba. I need to strap you onto the seat to make sure that you are secure. The surf is a little rough today." That sounded good. I knew I swam like a rock. I looked at Charles and said, "Thanks." After all, he was looking out for me and my safety. Charles put the Mae West life jacket on me, tightened down the straps and made sure it was placed on me both properly and securely.

Charles handed me a seven-foot rod and reel, a red Ambassador. On the 20-pound test line he placed a blue MirrOlure with three silver treble hooks. I thought this lure, a coastal classic with quality stainless steel hardware, natural 3-D eyes, gills and scales, and double dipped heat cured exterior life-like finish, patterns and colors would be irresistible to my prey. Charles looked back at me and said, "Bubba, get ready. This is where the action starts. This is what I've been telling you about. Look at the condition of the water. Look at the bait fish. I cannot wait for you to see what you are about to experience as if you were wade fishing with your own legs and feet in the surf." Howard began wading forward in front of Charles. Charles stepped away from me out of the Proline boat. He slowly let the rope out which was tethered from his waist to the nose of the Bass Buster. I started casting and reeling in, casting and reeling in.

Yet, no fish took my irresistible lure. I looked at Howard ahead and then at Charles. They were not having any luck either. Charles had let all the rope out. It was fully extended behind him. That was part of his plan to give me enough space between the Bass Buster and him for me to have the true experience of fishing with other men in the surf. Enough distance to cast in his direction without hitting him.

Then, without warning, a substantial wave in the surf caught the right side of the Bass Buster pontoon boat square sideways. The wave was parallel to the pontoons. The Bass Buster was forcibly thrown up on the right side. I was flipped up and over to the left along with it. I was upside down, strapped and trapped underneath the water. It never occurred to me that the bass fishing vessel was suitable for only inland bays and freshwater which remain relatively calm. With the speed of light, I thought how ironic that I might die fishing with my dear, thoughtful brother Charles in the surf and not from polio, pneumonia, or the complications of surgery.

When there is nothing else, I had learned to rely on faith. That faith was always found in reliance upon the Lord's Prayer. Under the water I held my breath and said the Lord's Prayer. Then, "God, please help me! Amen". As if the arms of an Angel had come down from Heaven and grasped the vessel, the Bass Buster and I were just as suddenly and unexpectedly flipped upright.

I was up in the air long enough to take a deep breath and yell to Charles for help. But Charles was upwind from me. There was no chance for him to hear me through the gale of the wind or the roar of the surf. Then, another wave hit the Bass Buster. I was again in the water under it, repeating the Lord's Prayer. Then, again as if lifted by the arms of an Angel, the Bass Buster was flipped upright. I took another breath and screamed at Charles, "Help!" Charles was looking ahead, oblivious to what was going on behind him. Five or six times, during what seemed like an eternity, I was flipped upside down and right side up.

Finally, Howard must have heard the lips of an Angel whisper in his ear, "Look back. One of you is in trouble. He needs help. God is not ready for him to come home."

Howard turned and looked back at Charles. Howard noticed the Bass Buster was upside down. I was nowhere to be seen. He was upwind from Charles and yelled, "Bubba's in trouble!" Charlie looked back. To his horror, the Bass Buster was upside down.

Charles rushed to the Bass Buster and flipped it and me upright. I was alive. I looked at him and gasped for air. Charles looked at me. He was relieved that I was alive but he knew how close I had come to drowning instead of experiencing the surf at its best as he intended.

That was it for my fishing in the surf like a healthy Emmott man armed with the folklore of generations and manly use of artificial lures. Charles pulled the Bass Buster up onto the shore and secured it with an anchor in the sand. Charles's job was done. My life had been saved. My job now was to dry out. Charles' remaining job was to catch the fish.

I have always been anal retentive. That's one of the requirements of becoming a successful attorney. I hate being unshaven. I hate being unclean. I hate being smelly. I do not like the icky, sticky feeling of sand under my clothes. As I dried out that afternoon, all I wanted to do was to go home, get in the shower, put on a pair of pajamas and get in bed. But I was 385 miles from Houston and 25 miles offshore of Louisiana. I did not say a complaining word to Charles. I continued to be a good sport. I was alive after all, wasn't I?

Dorothy had shopped for us and planned a dinner feast for us. Driftwood was gathered from the beach for the camp fire. Baked potatoes were wrapped in foil and cooked with the coals of an outdoor fire. Three big rib eye steaks were put on a grate on top of the fire and cooked to perfection. Medium rare with only salt and pepper. Plans had been made for us to eat on shore and then sleep on the boat. Get up in the morning; fish some more and head back to

Houston.

But I was not feeling well. I did not want to be carried from the boat to the shore. Instead, I remained on the boat. Charles and Howard brought me the food that I had no hunger for, but I ate a little anyway. A canopy was put over the boat for the evening's sleep in case it rained. The boat was secured by an anchor. Unfortunately, the boat was anchored downwind from the smoldering fire of drift wood. By three in the morning I had diarrhea and was vomiting. My rear end was over a bucket and my mouth was over the side of the boat. Moses may have suffered and wandered forty years in the desert, but I did my share of mental, physical and spiritual tribulations between the hours of 8:00pm and 6:00am the next morning. Chills, respiratory fatigue, diarrhea, and vomiting. If I had had my iPhone then like I have now, I would not have hesitated calling 911. I would have begged for a Life Flight Helicopter from Hermann Hospital to come pick me up.

At sunrise, the darkness of my fears ended. It was a glorious morning. I had made it through the night. Jesus arose from the dead on Easter Sunday. I was alive after a near crucifixion in the surf. God still had plans for me.

The conditions of the water were the same as the previous day. The bait fish were churning and rippling on the surface of the water. The fish we wanted to catch were knocking the bait fish out of the water in a feeding frenzy. In the Proline boat we each cast our lures. First, the MirrOlures. Then the Bingos. Then the silver spoons. Then the gold spoons. The trout, red fish, and mackerel had no desire for artificial bait. They clearly wanted the real thing. We did not have what they wanted and they had what we needed to use as bait instead of artificial lures.

Charles drove the boat around Little Gosher Island one

more time. Then we swung back toward Old Shell Beach. Although there were no fish in our ice box, I was very relieved we were finally headed home. All in one piece. All alive. We had made our passage through the ritual of the unprepared, the ridiculous, the untimely, and the non-catastrophic and miraculous Bass Buster incident. As Charles steered the boat back toward Old Shell Beach and as we rounded the western tip of Little Gosher Island, I looked back at Charles. I thought about how great it was to be headed home. We did not have our catch, but we still had each other.

Then a blessing occurred, of sorts. I looked back to the rear of the boat. As the motor purred, pushing the boat forward, a six-pound speckled trout jumped out of the water and into the back of the boat. It was as if God or an Angel said, "You are not leaving empty-handed after this!" Maybe it was God or the Angel who had saved me in the surf, giving us three a blessing—part of the feast that Charles had intended to give me. The Lord did not feed 5,000 that day. Just three hungry, empty-handed fishermen. We laughed in unison. We were one amidst the sun, the sand and the surf. Charlie grabbed the slippery six-pound trout with both hands and placed it into the ice box to be eaten later. The boat made its way into port. Charles and Howard fastened the tow line to the ring on the nose of the Proline boat. They pulled the boat up onto the trailer by taking turns cranking the handle to the wrench mounted to the front of the trailer.

It was Sunday morning about 11:00am. We stopped for some convenience-store fast food in the sleepy, slow-paced town of Old Shell Beach. Howard and Charles couldn't stand being stinky either. They both looked at me and said, "It's time to take a bath." I replied, "How can we do that? We have no money for a hotel or motel." Charles and Howard looked at each other and smiled.

I looked out my window. They had parked the car, boat and trailer in front of a car wash, which was located directly in front of the exit of a Catholic church. Sunday services were in progress. The church's parking lot was full. While the worship service was going on inside, Charles and Howard decided to be uncharacteristically irreverent and take a public bath at a time when every God loving and respectful person in the world would be doing something like that in private.

Charles said, "Bubba, do you have any quarters?" I had one. I asked him, "What do you want to do with it?" Charles did not answer. Howard said, "I've got three." Charles said, "Good. We need fifty cents for the soap cycle and fifty cents for the rinse cycle." I thought these two people had more sense than that. Then I thought they were just joking and playing a game on me. But as they took off their shoes and socks in the front seat of the car, and then their shirts and blue jeans, I knew that this was no joke. This joke would not be pulled on me. Charles and Howard, armed with the change for the soap and rinse cycles, exited the car. They were clad only in their t-shirts and underwear. As he exited, Charles said, "Don't worry. We have enough money for you too, Bubba. We'll be back for you in a few minutes."

I was appalled to see Charles and Howard sharing the car wash hose and nozzle. Howard shoved the hose and nozzle up his t-shirt and down his BVD underwear, and Charles did the same to himself. If anyone asked me at that moment whether I knew these two people I would have denied it. I would have denied them like Peter denied Jesus at Pilate's house.

With the soap cycle completed, it was time for the rinse. Charles and Howard repeated the outlandish ritual one more time. That kind of cleanliness was not Godliness. By that time, I had staked my ground. Every door in the car was locked. Every window was raised up. I planned to fight to the death to keep from experiencing the embarrassment I had witnessed them commit on the outside of my automotive fortress.

My shame and embarrassment for them grew greater as I noticed the line of cars of faithful worshippers exiting the Catholic Church's parking lot and passing by my underwear-clad brother and cousin. The windows of the cars framed the stoic but incredulous stares of the women looking at Charles and Howard. They probably thought these two young men were drunk. They were not drunk. I can assure you that. They were just crazy enough to bathe in public in a car wash in front of a church in the Deep South on the most holy day of the week, right before the eyes of God and his faithful flock.

I unlocked the door and let Howard and Charles in after they made a promise not to put me through another ordeal. Good for me and good for them, they kept their word. I preferred to sit stinky in the backseat of the car all the way home than to be wild and free and irreverent like them.

Seven and a half hours later, Charles pulled the car into the driveway and turned me over to Dorothy. She saw to it that I got a hug, a bath, a little supper, my pajamas and a soft pillow under my head in my own bed. A few evenings later, Charles, Dorothy, Howard and I feasted on that six-pound trout.

Although over the years, Charles has been the brunt of much teasing and joking about this "trip of a lifetime" he gave his brother, Bubba, my love and respect for him were never diminished because of this fishing trip. Like a good brother, his intentions for me were only good. His purposes were Divine. Not everything turns out in life like we plan. Charlie's love gave me something to look back on and laugh about and appreciate for more than forty years. Because of Charles, we were blessed with fish to eat. The arms of an Angel righted the boat. An Angel's lips were heard by Howard in order to save my life. I remained blessed with a brother, Charles, who gave me a trip of a lifetime and who did his best to allow me to experience what it felt like to fish in the surf in the most unforgettable way.

As I reflect on my journey with Charles and our challenges with polio, I am thankful Charles' eyes have said so much to me in our years together. As if they were words from his lips, his eyes said, "My heart is strong. Yet it hurts for you. My heart was with you as I stood in the circle driveway at Hedgecroft Hospital and looked up at you in the second story window as the nurse held you up to look down at me and Carolyn Jean. It hurt me to see the nurse had to hold your arm up and wave your hand at me. I could not understand why I could not come upstairs to see you. You being quarantined was the same as me being imprisoned from embracing your pain, from helping you heal with my own hands."

My Angel Charles used his legs and arms and heart to enable me to live, to grow, and to experience my own limits accompanied by an uncritical, non-judgmental, and accepting brother.

As I sit at the head table with Dorothy at our fortieth wedding anniversary celebration, my brother, Charles, takes the podium. He is having difficulty expressing his thoughts on this auspicious occasion. He speaks from his heart with his hallmark care. It is obvious to me that he has given much thought to his remarks.

As he speaks, I see at the same time a brother of 63 and

my little brother of 5 when I was struck down by polio. Charles surprises me. He says he has regrets. I do too. He is apologetic about not always being there for me, especially after high school when he sojourned to Louisiana to sell pots, pans and knives. I feel badly about not always being there for him too. He says that although he knew I was chasing my dreams by marrying Dorothy and going off to law school at UT in 1972, he felt as though he had lost me once again as he did in 1954 to polio.

Although he had done so much for me, Charles never felt it was enough. He expressed that he always needed me more than I ever needed him.

Nothing could be farther from the truth.

No, Charlie, you were never left behind. We both won. We both lost. We both gained. You never left me. I never left you.

Together we learned, from the ages of five and six, a very important lesson. Life is not fair. It is simply…a gift. Part of that simple, precious gift came with a sweet, devoted, beloved brother, Charles, with an angelic heart. Our mother, Lucile, knows that God's call to you as her disciple to care for me has been fulfilled. May God continue to bless you and uplift your wings to Heaven for you are my Best Man, my best friend, and my Angel Brother. Amen.

CHAPTER 13

My Mother, An Angel in Disguise

Dearest Mother, You were God's greatest blessing to me, a son given to you, yet also partially snatched away by paralysis, debilitating surgeries, endless physical therapy, and countless other challenges.

When I think of you, Mother, I think about your entire life as prayer. How the sacred was seen in the ordinary things you did and said to all of us, in your sweet and extraordinary ways. Your inexhaustible joy in taking good care of others.

Mom, I have always loved hearing the story of how you and Dad met in Austin, Texas in May 1941. Dad said you were the "beautiful brunette" next door; you said he was the "good looking" fraternity boy in the SigEp house next to the house where you rented a room. Remember that intense game of horseshoes that he and his friend began playing right after seeing you pinning up your wash on the backyard clothes line? Later, you would find out that they were playing each other for the privilege of asking you for a first date. Luckily, Dad won. You later told me he looked like a Prince Charming on that night's date in his double-breasted suit. Your face would light up when you talked about your own outfit of high heels, a stylish hat, and a dress your mother had sewn.

I've often wondered how you made it through your younger life, Mother. Your father died of tuberculosis that same year, in 1941, after years of fighting TB through quarantines and hospitalizations. He didn't even see you graduate from high school. Your own mother was left with a son of 21, yourself at 18, and your two younger sisters, age 16 and 14. You didn't know some of the other wartime hardships you and Dad would endure: your own mother's death of pneumonia in mid-1942 only a few months after your marriage to Dad, the four years that you and Dad would be separated during the War, the tragedy of your first pregnancy ending in the stillborn death of a baby girl, while Dad was preparing to leave for the European Campaign.

But, Mother, what I most cherish about the life you and Dad made for us is how you brought us all into a life of prayer centered around the ordinary events of each day. You made sure that all of us were home for dinner around the table with Dad saying Grace before the meals. You made sure that we all knelt at bedtime with you to say the Lord's Prayer. All of the holidays, such as Easter and Christmas, were centered on first gathering to pray at church, then gathering the extended family to exquisite, seated meals at your overflowing formal table.

Mom, you also showed us the importance of worship. Every Sunday morning you dressed us in our very best clothes. I saw the love and pride on your face as you looked at all of us. Mom, I have to tell you that even though I liked Sunday school for a while, I preferred staying in the church with you and Dad. When I was younger, I admit that I didn't understand a lot of the words in the sermon. But being in the nave of St. Francis Episcopal Church, where I listened to the beautiful hymns sung by the choir in the loft and the organ playing, and your lovely voice, Mother, introduced me to song as worship. As you held the Hymnal for me to read and sing with you, I saw the white gloves on your hands, the hat and veil you wore on your head. I thanked God in church for giving you to me.

You were the most beautiful woman on earth to me, your small son. You still are, Mother.

The faith you had in God and His Angels has served me well, Mother. Once I was running a high fever—at eight years old. You had rubbed Vicks Vapor Rub on my chest and covered me with a T-shirt. A vaporizer was running so that I could breathe easier. I was laying on my right side with my head on the pillow. I felt a strangely ominous, fore-boding presence. I rolled over on my back and looked to my left. I saw a figure that looked like Satan leaning against the bedroom wall facing me. He was smiling at me and had pointed ears and a pitchfork. His face and eyes said, "I am ready to take you with me." I didn't call you or Dad for help or even scream out of fear. I just rolled over on my right side, closed my eyes and said the Lord's Prayer over and over and over again asking God to rid my room of Satan. After a few prayers, I rolled back over. Satan was gone. You see, Mother, I don't know whether it was Satan or a fever-in-duced hallucination. What mattered was the presence and power of prayer. What mattered was that God saved me at the moment of terror. I learned to have this faith from you, Mother. What an incalculable blessing.

And Mom, there were the practical lessons in how to live life. You know, those lessons like: "If you can't say something nice, don't say anything at all," and "Leave things the way you found them," and "Don't steal."

I'll never forget how you imparted this last lesson to me. Once, when I was four, you took me to one of those sprawling, white ranch-style homes off Memorial Drive. While you were inside raising money for a charity, I noticed that there was a beautiful, red plastic lawnmower in the front yard. Now, I didn't have one of these at our house. I just knew I could mow the lawn outside your kitchen window with this one, and you would be so proud of me. So while you were inside, I opened the back door of our 1952 Oldsmobile, folded the lawnmower and placed it behind the front seat. When we got home, you said "Bubba, you want to come in with me?" "No, Mom, I want to stay outside." You walked inside and closed the door. A few minutes later you looked out the window and saw me mowing the yard with the beautiful red plastic lawnmower. The way you looked at me through that window let me know I was in big trouble. You rushed out the door and asked, "Bubba, where did you get that lawnmower?" "From that nice lady's house, Mama." "Bubba, get that lawnmower, put it in the car. We are going over there right now. Stealing is wrong. You took what was not yours. God says stealing is a sin. You must return the lawnmower, apologize, and then you must pray to God tonight for the forgiveness of your sin."

Mom, I still recall how mortified I was to stand at the front door of that house and return that lawnmower and apologize. After I did that, you didn't make me feel any better by taking me to buy my own plastic mower. Somehow you knew that in those moments kids need parents not friends.

Mom, there were also life lessons in the quietness of our lives. Those times I didn't realize until decades later were teaching us intangible lessons. Remember how you used to have us kids polish the silver for hours before important family dinners? We grumbled and wished we could be doing something else. But later I came to understand that you were showing us that it's important to be attentive to the little details of life—to take the time and effort to create beauty by attending to the small things. See, Mom, you knew that we would come to love the beauty of a gloriously set table which we had contributed to by our own scrubbing and polishing. You knew it would calm our spinning minds and give us memorable times in the warm kitchen with you. I can hear your voice reminding me that a lot of little things in life are not seen, appreciated, or rewarded until much later. What Charles, Carolyn Jean, and I did with the silver polish, soft cloth, and hard work made the tarnish disappear. We saw instantly how to contribute to beauty. Mom, you taught us that life is a lot like that. Little actions produce big results. Small things matter—more than we know.

Mother, how many times did you save my life? Remember when you summoned Father Daubert to Hedgecroft Hospital in the fall of 1954? I had pneumonia. My breathing was labored and supported by a respirator. My bed and body were canopied by an oxygen tent. Dr. Montgomery had told you and Dad that my death was near. I recall looking from the bed past the clear plastic wall of the tent. In the darkness, Father Daubert and you, my sad but faithful Mother, held open prayer books. During the Last Rites you noticed I was turning blue. You interrupted the priest to have my oxygen tank checked. It was empty. If you had not stopped the Last Rites, I surely would have died.

In so many other ways, Mother, you also saved my life. You did not let me crawl into a shell and withdraw from the world. You made sure I stayed connected, although at times I felt out of place in the world because of polio. When I had surgery at the age of 11 and had three steel rods put in my back, you did not allow me to stay at home and miss the family reunion. You put shoes and socks on my feet, and my yellow shorts and a T-shirt over my upper body cast. You had given me a burr haircut that summer, much to my chagrin. The last place I wanted to be was lying on a cot at the base of a sprawling oak tree at the site of the family reunion with that ugly haircut. But, Mom, like those other times, it turned out the better for me. All afternoon, as I lay on that cot at the base of the tree, my cousin Mary Lou, who was about 16, sat on a blanket on the ground next to me. She talked with me and told me entertaining stories. She also narrated what was going on around us. At times, she sat silently with me. It is amazing how beautiful that day was and how healing it was for me years later. Mom, I wish I still had that picture of Mary Lou and me under the oak tree that hot summer afternoon. It was lost in a flood or is buried in a box somewhere.

Mom, do you remember the surgery I had in 1964 right before I started high school? I had broken a rod in my back. Dr. Paul Harrington had replaced the rod. I found myself with that hated burr haircut, again, on a cot. Just before school started there was a dance for all the students from the two junior highs who would be attending Cy-Fair High School. I gave you unmitigated hell. I did not want to go. I did not feel acceptable. I couldn't move around. I couldn't dance. I would not know half the people there. I was very depressed, too. Yet, you wouldn't take no for an answer. You put me on a cot and loaded me in the back of the Ford Fairlane station wagon. You and Dad and others carried me into the gym where the dance was being held. Below the streamers which hung from the walls of the gym and the crepe-papered rims of the basketball goals, the ends of my cot were placed on two metal chairs. During the evening, my fellow students came over and greeted me. One sweet girl, Linda Wichkoski, sat with me for most of the evening. Years later, I realized how much she had wanted to make me feel comfortable and how she probably, too, felt out of place and awkward.

And, most of all, Mother, I want to thank you for never setting limits on what I could be and become. You never sought to rescue me from seeking "unrealistic" goals. You never told me that God would not cure me. You never told me I would not make a full recovery from polio. You never told me that I would not make the baseball team and be Wonder Boy Emmott. You never told me that I would not make the marching band or the football team. You never told me I could not be an attorney nor have a wife and children. You never told me there wasn't someone out there who would see me and think that I was still a handsome man despite my scars and deformities. And when I did fall or suffer disappointments, you were always there to pick me up, to brush me off, to sit with me in my pain, and to cry with me.

When you married Dad and gave birth to Carolyn Jean, Charles, and me, your three oldest children, I know you had much different plans. With polio those plans changed in many ways. Just as you never allowed me to crawl into a dark shell and remain in hopelessness and just as you never gave up on me or what I could become, as a miracle of sorts, you never gave up on God. Your hope and faith in God did not become casualties of my polio. You never lost either. Life went on.

It would have been easy and somewhat understandable for you to have lost your hope and to have given up on

God. How could He do this after all you had been through and had lost? How could your son not be cured considering your faith, your prayers and your service as a sister in Christ? How could you now be expected to be a wife and mother to two more sons, Gary and Russell, and continue to serve others, to travel away from me with Dad, to have fellowship with life-long friends, or to play bridge with your ladies? But you held on to hope and kept your faith in God.

In you, Mom, and in your precious birth, God surely set a light of love to shine not only on me but also on a much larger world. A world more significant and unbounded than muscles which could no longer move or bones that were no longer straight. There were the things you did regardless. Celebration of birthdays – baptisms – weddings – confirmations. Observation of the seasons of our Church such as Advent, Christmas, Lent, Easter. You had a bigger life. Family reunions. Lawn parties. Dancing with friends under lights hanging from the trees in our front yard. You had a love of life you were determined to live. Every single day you climbed over a wall of worry and showed me that with God, enduring faith and prayer, all things were indeed possible. All your tears as my mother never drowned the hope of the Christ Child or diminished the power of prayer. You made sure that no day was so dark that the faith of a mother and her son could not see the Light and Grace of God's Love or the Divine presence of His Angels among us.

Mother, I can never repay you. It is no coincidence that a child like me stricken with polio was given such an extraordinary mother by God. I might be responsible for many things, but God gave you as a gift to me. In the sacredness of His Holy gift, you were always totally devoted to me. You never once complained that I was a burden or that you were tired. It was as if you had proclaimed to God, "Polio is no match for me. Bring on the bedpans, the urinals, the soiled sheets, the incisions to dress, the therapy exercises to do with my son's paralyzed limbs. I am your servant. I do this work in Your Name and in the Glory of your Grace."

I love you, Mother. My first love. My first Bending Angel.

You are my first and sweetest memory. I am lying on my back in a baby bassinet surrounded by white wicker. I look up and see the bright radiance of the sunlight shining through the window in front of me. In the light above me I see the silhouette of a fair, dark-haired figure bending over me. She places her warm hands under me. She carefully lifts me up and cradles me in her arms. She gently holds me close to her warm chest. I look up into my mother's eyes. I see an Angel in disguise.

CHAPTER FOURTEEN

Thanks Be to God

The Thirteen Bending Angels of this book are thirteen chapters in the book of my life. Thirteen Holy Messengers of God's eternal light and love for me. As with the gift of His Son, the Risen Christ, each of God's Angels were His gift to me. I did not earn them. Just as I did not "earn" infantile paralysis.

Just as the five wounds of Christ were healed by God's love for Him, that same Divine, never-ending love for me transformed all my missing parts, through prayer, into a better reflection of the boy He ensouled and He intended me to become at my birth.

Almighty God, today I sit with a pen in my weak right hand, but with a stronger faith in You. I have a deep belief that Your Angels are here now. That I have had more than thirteen encounters with living Angels. That the Bending Angel painted by Charles Schorre invited me to have a closer relationship with You and Your Son, Jesus Christ.

Because of these Angels. Because of You. Because of prayer. I am living in You.

Lord, I give You thanks and praise for sending me these

living Angels when I needed Your love and protection the most. I pray that You help me in how I walk my faith. With my feet standing firmly on the earth You made for me and with my heart in heaven, may I hear the voices of Your Angels who bend over me and those I love. May I find, in the simple and ordinary, the Messengers of Your love, and, thereby, find You, Most Gracious Heavenly Father.

Amen.

Bending Angels: Living Messengers of God's Love is another **Bending Angel Project.**

As with his first book of prayers, *Prayerful Passages: Asking God's Help in Reconciliation, Separation, and Divorce,* these works are born from the inspiration received by author Jack H. Emmott from a painting he purchased at a charity art show in the 1990s. This painting of a Bending Angel was created by renowned Texas Artist of the Year, the late Charles Schorre.

The mission of **Bending Angel Projects** is to invite Christians through prayer, story, poetry, music and art to more fully experience the love and presence of God and His Angels.

Coming soon is the *Companion Guidebook* co-authored by Jack H. Emmott and Sarah Cortez for use with *Prayerful Passages: Asking God's Help in Reconciliation, Separation, and Divorce.* Through Biblical references and prayerful exercises contained in the *Companion Guidebook,* individuals, couples, lay and Christian church leaders will explore unseen and unexpected ways to improve or save marriages.

For those couples who suffer the devastating and guilt-ridden loss of marriage due to divorce, the *Companion Guidebook* will lead heartbroken people to a loving, nurturing and healing light filled place. Marriages may have begun at weddings and ended in divorce. But fortunately God and His love are forever. Look for the publication date at www.BendingAngel.com.

Jack H. Emmott has created a line of **Bending Angel** notecards and stationary so that you can send an inspired beautiful angel with your handwritten messages.

Jack encourages you, his reader, to spend more time in prayer and to be a part of what he refers to as slow living and mindful loving for Christ.

In the hurried and harried pace of the digital world you can bring heaven nearer to earth by taking time to pen a personal note to one who is loved, to give thanks and praise, to send healing words or a handwritten prayer to one who is grieving or is ill. Time will pass more slowly. You may become someone else's angel or you may find he or she has become yours.

Bending Angel notecards are the perfect reminder that heart-felt communications are a way we become angels in the lives of others. These folded blank cards on 100# paper in six assorted colors let you express your love, your concern, your joy to the receiver.

For ordering and product details and to hear about the future release of other stationary, please visit **www.BendingAngel.com.**